KT-394-144

For Ayno, Milos & Uma

PROLOGUE

Agnes came out of her bedroom. She had put on make-up, done her hair and prettified herself for me. Her daughters, standing beside her, were pleased to see their mother like that.

'It's your visitor from Europe,' they told her. 'The grandson.'

'Who?' she asked, in slightly too loud a voice.

'You know, the grandson.' But Agnes didn't know; I could see that from her face.

We greeted one another, and sat down at her circular living-room table somewhere in Buenos Aires. I knew Agnes from my grandmother's diary, the journal that I had with me in my bag. They had grown up together in a tiny village in the west of Hungary, seeing each other every day as children, although their lives were very different. Agnes's parents kept a delicatessen shop, my grandmother's parents owned a small castle. There was a courtyard with a gravel surface and a chestnut tree growing in the middle of it. *We lived a quiet life in the country,* my grandmother wrote about her childhood, *a life determined by the seasons of the year.* Until the war.

Until a day in the spring of 1944 when the well-ordered routine of centuries disappeared from that village, and with it a whole world. First came the Germans, then the Russians. The castle burned down, my grandmother's family lost all their land, their status, their place in society.

And Agnes was sent to Auschwitz.

I was just passing through, that was how her family had prepared Agnes for my visit, telling her that I had found information concerning her in a diary. 'About your parents,' they said, about a time seventy years ago. And now, they told her, I was here to read her a few extracts from it.

'How wonderful,' she said.

Sitting beside Agnes, I could see the number tattooed on her arm by a guard in Auschwitz. It was disappearing into the folds of her wrinkled skin now, leaving the figures barely legible. 802 . . . 6? Or was that an 8?

'Apple or curd cheese?' I was asked.

'What?'

Agnes was eighteen when she was deported to the concentration camp; today she is over ninety. Her walking frame stood within reach, beside her chair. I saw photographs on a small shelf: her late husband, the weddings of her daughters, a whole life.

'Apple, please,' I said, holding out my plate. And when we had all eaten our slices of strudel, I began reading aloud: about the train from Budapest, how you could see it coming a long way off because of the cloud of sooty smoke it puffed out – here Agnes nodded; about the cranes on the way into the village; the cherries preserved in syrup that stood beside the cash desk in her parents' shop; about her father Herr Mandl, who had such red cheeks.

'Oh yes, so he did,' she interrupted me cheerfully, and we all rejoiced with her, although none of us felt like it. Because we knew the truth.

*

A day later, in the Departures lounge at the airport, I asked myself: have we done the right thing? Apart from a man with a cleaning trolley, going from one end of the terminal to the other and leaving alternate darker and lighter stripes on the carpet flooring, there was no one else around, not a human soul in sight.

I'm only the messenger, I had persuaded myself before flying out. I have something that belongs to Agnes, that was why I had come, but now I wasn't so sure. Was I really only a courier?

Seven years had passed since I first set out to track down my family's wartime secrets. I had been to Hungary several times, and to Austria; I had flown to Russia, and now to Buenos Aires. But above all, I was now the father of three children, which made everything more complicated: I had learnt to change nappies and blend baby food, and I had found out about my roots; I spent days in a little place called Rechnitz to discover more about a massacre of 180 Jews, I trudged through Siberian snow in search of the remains of a labour camp, and finally I ended up in South America. I discussed all this every week with my psychoanalyst in Zürich. While other people were lunching on pizza, we talked about Stalin, the Holocaust and mass graves. Only recently I had asked him, 'Do you think I'm genuinely sick?' To which he replied, 'How would I know?'

It felt like living in a time machine that merged yesterday with today. I travelled from the past to the present, looking down at myself from above as I moved around my biographical axis. Seven years. That's about the life expectancy of European moles. I read a good deal about those animals in my grandmother's diary, because she was always comparing herself with them.

So I sat in the Departures lounge looking out, I saw runways black with rubber, and beyond them dingy fields, the great expanses of Argentina.

Agnes's daughters had given me a slim volume by their mother when we said goodbye, her memoir of the war years, and it was now in my bag with my grandmother's diary. The life stories of two dissimilar women, intermingling and foreshadowing the present. I was leafing through them. All we need now is my own story, I thought, taking my notebook out of my jacket, smoothing a new page, and writing the date in the top left-hand corner: *October 2013*.

What am I going to write, I wondered, a letter? Who to – to myself? How do you begin a letter like that?

Then my flight was called.

1

It all began one Thursday in April, about seven years before my
visit to Buenos Aires. At the time I was working for the Sunday
edition of the *Neue Zürcher Zeitung*. It was early in the morning,
when there was hardly anyone in the office, and all was calm. I was
writing a column about a sperm donor from the Netherlands when
a rather older woman colleague, who seldom had much to say to me,
put a page of newsprint down on my desk and said, 'That's quite
some family you have, don't you?'

I glanced up and smiled at her. Only then did I look at the article
she had torn out of the paper to show me. I was expecting something
to do with the 19th century, elaborate period dresses maybe, or
horses. Some bridge or other named after one of my forebears, an
Àdám, Zsigmund or Ladislaus Batthyány; my surname is well known
in Hungary. The Batthyánys had been counts, princes, bishops. One
of them was prime minister of the country in 1849, another, Ladislaus Batthyány-Strattmann, was beatified in 2003 by Pope John Paul
II for his services to Rome as a medical doctor. The family history
can be followed back to the Turkish wars of the 14th century, although
here in the West few people know the name, and why should they?
They generally think it is Tamil, because the two letters 'y' in it sug-
gest Sri Lanka. I get asked about it only during the Christmas
holidays, when they show the trilogy of films about Sissi, the Empress Elisabeth of Austria, on TV at eleven in the morning, and the
Empress, played by Romy Schneider, dances with a Count Batthyány

who wears a baby-blue uniform and has a large amount of brilliantine on his hair.

So I expected something like that when I glanced at the newspaper, something harmless. Instead, I read the headline 'The Hostess From Hell', which I didn't understand, but I recognized the woman in the photograph at once. Aunt Margit. The story said that in March, 1945, she had taken part in the massacre of 180 Jews in the Austrian border town of Rechnitz. Apparently she had thrown a party, with dancing and drinking, and at midnight, for fun, the guests held pistols to the heads of naked Jews, men and women alike, and pulled the triggers.

'Thanks,' I said, putting the sheet of newsprint aside and returning to the cursor blinking on my screen. I still had two hours before handing in my piece about the Dutch sperm donor.

Aunt Margit? My great-aunt with the pointed tongue?

When I was a child, we went to have lunch with Aunt Margit three times a year, always at the most expensive restaurant in Zürich. My father chain-smoked in our white Opel all the way, my mother combed my hair with a plastic comb. We called her Aunt Margit, never just Margit, as if 'Aunt' were a title. She had married my father's uncle, but the marriage was disastrous from the first. Margit was a billionaire from the German Thyssen family. She was tall, with a large torso and thin legs. In my memory she always wears a skirt suit with the jacket buttoned up to her throat, and silk scarves with horse patterns on them; her crocodile handbag is claret-coloured with gold clasps, and when she talks about deer in the rutting season or cruising in the Aegean, she puts out the tip of her tongue like a lizard in the pauses between sentences. I sit as far away as possible from her. Aunt Margit hated children, and while I push chopped calves' liver around my plate I keep looking at her. I want to see that tongue.

After her death we seldom mentioned her, and my memories of

our lunches faded, until the day when I read the report in the paper about that little place in Austria. Rechnitz. About a party. About a massacre. About 180 Jews who had to strip naked before they were shot, so that their bodies would decompose more quickly. And Aunt Margit? She was at the centre of it.

I phoned my father and asked him if he knew about the party. He said nothing for a while, and I heard him uncorking a bottle of wine. I saw him in my mind's eye, sitting on the shabby old sofa that I like so much in his living-room in Budapest.

'Margit had a couple of affairs with Nazis, there was talk about that in the family.'

'It says in the paper that she threw a party, and the high point, as a kind of treat for dessert, was when 180 Jews were lured into a stable and guns were handed out to the guests, who were all dead drunk. They all joined in, Margit too. She's described as the hostess from Hell. The English newspapers are calling her the "killer count-ess". And there's a picture of her captioned: "Thyssen countess had 200 Jews shot at Nazi party"'.

'Nonsense. Yes, a crime was committed, but I think it's unlikely that Margit was involved. She was a monster, but not capable of doing that.'

'How come Margit was a monster?'

*

Before I read that newspaper story about Rechnitz and Aunt Margit, I hadn't been especially interested in my family's history. I had little contact with it. If I had been born in Hungary it would have been different; there were places and monuments there with connections to my ancestors. However, I grew up not in Buda-pest but in a four-roomed apartment on the outskirts of the city of Zürich, and when I was eight we moved a hundred metres fur-ther away to a grey town house shaped like a Rubik's cube, the puzzle that everyone played with back in the eighties. We had a ping-pong table in the garden, and a large American-style fridge that the previous occupants had left behind. It smelled so good when you opened the freezer compartment and put your head right in, past the frozen peas. I remember, even more vividly, the smell of the fuel station where we sometimes stopped on the way back from visiting friends of my parents. My two brothers and I used to sit squeezed together on the back seat, and I always hoped the tank would need filling. Then I would wind down the car window, close my eyes and breathe in through my nose. The petrol and the cool air, and all of us together in that car on the way home – I never felt safer in my life. And when we arrived I would pretend to be asleep, so that my father would carry me into my room, with his shirt still smelling of wine and cigarettes and summer. It was all part of my childhood.

Like whales who make for calm waters when they are about to give birth, my parents had withdrawn from the outside world to settle here. But unlike whales, who then return to the ocean depths, my parents remained stranded on the outskirts of the city.

Maybe they were hiding from their past. From their memories of Hungary, of the war, of flight and concealment.

Or possibly they simply wanted to begin again in this undefiled place. Rather than thinking back to earlier times, they wanted to make this dead-end spot their home. And it almost worked.

Switzerland is a good country for beginning again and shedding the burden of the past; there is nothing in it to remind you of Hitler or Stalin. The two totalitarian systems of the last century, National Socialism and Communism, the concentration camps and the gulag, are only chapters in school history books to the Swiss. There are hardly any memorials to the victims of wars, hardly any families, apart from those of immigrants, whose stories are interwoven with those atrocities. People don't ask, 'Grandpa, what did you do in the war?' No one in Switzerland was deported or gassed. There's nothing that the Swiss have to 'stomach', there is nothing to 'come out', as the newspapers always say about revelations in other countries. There was no collective failure, there were no crises outside the world of banking. Switzerland has known only years of prosperity and security; the minds of the Swiss were at ease, particularly in my youth at the beginning of the nineties, when everything was even brighter than before, and people living in city suburbs would get on their bikes at weekends and cycle out to the lakes.

You might expect the colour of such an idyll to rub off on its surroundings. You might expect such carefree attitudes to transfer themselves to a family's fortunes. It isn't always like that.

Neither my father nor my mother really felt at home in Switzerland, that most comfortably padded of all European countries. They did learn to speak Swiss German, they went skiing, they bought a sandwich toaster when everyone was buying them, and in winter they ate *raclette* like everyone else, pouring melted cheese over potatoes, maybe adding a little extra paprika. But the fact is that they participated in the life of the country only when they had to. They exchanged civil greetings with their neighbours, but they would rather get to their car unseen by any acquaintances. In secret, Switzerland and the Swiss smiled at that, or so at least it seemed to me earlier. My parents weren't bothered by the occasional xenophobic remarks of other inhabitants of Zürich – what a funny surname we had, we spoke German pretty well for foreigners, our rusty car didn't really suit this city – because they knew that they were never going to put down roots there. As they saw Switzerland, it was never more than a toy country, life there wasn't the genuine article, or at least not real life with its ups and downs, with its joy and grief. Because no one who had not at least lost a few relations in the war, who had not known what it was to see a foreign power, whether German or Russian, turn everything upside down, could truly claim to understand life. Suffering was the common currency.

Idyllic happiness counted for nothing. The past was always more important than the future, old was always better than modern.

And so they probably dreamed of another life in their own way, in that little house on the outskirts of Zürich, a city without yesterdays from which my father soon moved.

Two years after the Iron Curtain came down, he packed his bags and went to Budapest. My mother also left Switzerland, and did not seem to feel that she was missing anything. I never bore her a grudge for that. All of a sudden they were both gone, but they had left me with a sense that I was living in the wrong country.

I stayed where I was, all the same, perhaps out of inertia; studied at university, because that was what everyone did, and became a journalist. Soon I was writing about armed gangs of kids in Liverpool, I slept in the caravan belonging to a high-ranking Ku Klux Klan member in Texas, I spent several days walking around the streets of a Zürich suburb to report on the case of a girl of thirteen who had been gang-raped, and I sat on the Dutch sperm donor's sofa with a lesbian couple who wanted a child. I saw him give them a small container and a syringe, so that one of them could inject herself with his sperm. 'I'm just going out to do a bit of shopping,' he called, already in the doorway. 'Do you want anything? Cola? Crisps?' The women shook their heads, taken aback. Cola? It was a baby that they wanted.

Hungary might be my parents' country, but what business of mine was that? I was in my early thirties, newly in love. The Second World War and a war crime involving the murder of 180 Jews couldn't have been farther away. We had our own problems, I thought, immigration, disorientation, globalization, I wrote about such subjects: too much consumption, too much pornography, too many opportunities.

But after coming up against my family history on the morning when I recognized Aunt Margit in the newspaper article, I began to do some research. I wrote to members of our family in Vienna, Budapest and Munich. 'Hello,' I began my letters. 'We haven't met, but we're distant relations. Have you read what's said to have happened? Do you know anything about it?' I got hold of files on Aunt Margit and her husband Ivan, my grandfather's brother; I read books about the Thyssens, the history of Hungary; I spent whole days in archives in Berlin and Berne, Budapest and Graz; and I had many conversations with my father. Aunt Margit had set me travelling back into past history: because of her, I faced the story of my origins for the first time in my life.

It was the massacre of 180 Jews that brought me closer to my family.

2

On a Sunday in the spring of 2008 I went to Rechnitz for the first time, to find out what my aunt really had to do with the crime. I arrived in Vienna first thing in the morning, on the night train from Zürich, hired a car, and drove past woods and vineyards; the grapes on the vines were still small and hard. Rechnitz is no beauty spot, there's not much more to it than a main street, lined to right and left by low-roofed houses with narrow windows, curtained to keep out prying eyes. There is no town centre, no market place, and the castle that the immensely rich industrialist and art collector Heinrich Thyssen left in his will to his daughter Margit, our Aunt Margit, no longer stands. In 1945 the Russians bombed it when they marched into Austria, whereupon the inhabitants left, taking all the furniture, the pictures and the carpets with them. The Refugius association organizes an annual commemoration service for the murdered Jews. Songs are sung and prayers said at the Kreuzstadl, a historic ruin on the way into the town that is now preserved as a memorial. The speeches made in 2008 repeated that the crime must never be forgotten. I stood a little way to one side, knowing no one there, and looked around. The sun was shining, dandelions were in flower, the grass was ankle-high and still a little damp. Somewhere under it, 180 skulls lay buried. In spite of many years of searching for it, the mass grave has not been found to this day.

*

The night between 24 and 25 March 1945 is bright with moonlight. A party for Nazis and their hangers-on is being held in Margit

Batthyány-Thyssen's castle in Rechnitz in the Burgenland district, near the Austro-Hungarian border. Members of the Gestapo and local Nazi bigwigs, like SS-Hauptscharführer Franz Podezin, like Josef Muralter and Hans-Joachim Oldenburg, are talking to members of the Hitler Youth and the castle staff, while they drink sparkling wine. The National Socialists know that the war is lost and the Russians have already reached the Danube, but that is not allowed to cast a pall over the festive atmosphere. It is eight in the evening. At the same time, about 200 Jewish forced labourers from Hungary are standing on Rechnitz railway station. They have been working on the construction of the south-east rampart, a huge fortified line of defence intended to run from Poland by way of Slovakia and Hungary to Trieste and hold back the advancing Red Army. At nine-thirty in the evening, the truck driver Franz Ostermann tells some of the Jews to get into his truck, and after a short drive hands them over to four SA men, who give the prisoners shovels and tell them to dig an L-shaped pit.

The Hungarian Jews begin digging; they are tired and weak, the ground is hard, there is much drinking and dancing in Aunt Margit's castle. About nine o'clock, SS Hauptscharführer Franz Podezin receives a phone call. The party is so noisy that he has to go into the next room to take the call, which lasts less then two minutes. Podezin concludes it by saying, 'Yes, yes!' and adds, 'What a bloody mess!' He tells Hildegard Stadler, head of the local branch of the League of German Girls, to take about ten to thirteen of the party guests into another room. 'The Jews from the railway station,' he tells them, 'are sick with typhoid fever and have to be shot.' No one demurs. Karl Muhr, the ordnance officer, hands out guns and ammunition to the guests. It is just after eleven o'clock. Three cars are ready in the castle courtyard; there isn't room for the whole group, so some walk. It isn't far.

*

I phoned my father. 'You knew Aunt Margit was there that night,' I told him, 'and you knew about the massacre, too.'

13

'Yes.'

'But did it never occur to you that she might have been involved in it?'

'Is this an interrogation?'

'Only asking.'

'I never thought there could be any connection between the party and the massacre, no, not the stuff they're saying in the papers these days. Wait a moment.' He coughed, and I heard him take a cigarette out of its packet.

'You smoke too much.'

'How's the little one?'

'She's getting her third tooth and crawling. How come you never discussed the war with Aunt Margit?'

'What would you have expected me to ask her? Can I give you a little more wine, Aunt Margit? Oh, and by the way, Aunt Margit, did you ever shoot any Jews?'

'Yes.'

'Don't be naïve. Those were courtesy visits. We used to talk about the weather, and she pulled various members of the family to pieces. "Rotten seed," that was how she described the Thyssens and the Batthyánys, she thought they were all out of their minds. "Rotten seed." It was her favourite saying. Do you remember that tongue of hers?'

*

Between midnight and three in the morning, Franz Ostermann makes seven journeys in all from the station to the Kreuzstadl, each time with 30 to 40 Jews in his truck, and hands them over to the four SA men. The Jews are ordered to undress and leave their clothes beside the pit. They kneel, naked, on the edge of their L-shaped grave. Podezin and Oldenburg stand there, fanatical Nazis both. They shoot the Jews in the backs of their necks. As Josef Muralter, a Nazi Party member, pulls the trigger he shouts, 'You bastards will burn! Traitors to the Fatherland!' The Jews collapse, fall into the pit, and lie there stacked on one another. More bottles of sparkling wine are being opened in the castle, someone is playing the accordion. Margit is young and likes to have fun, she wears the most beautiful clothes. A waiter called Viktor notices that at three in the morning, when the guests return to the hall where the party is being held, they are gesticulating wildly and their faces are flushed. SS Hauptscharführer Podezin, who has just been shooting men and women in the head, is now dancing with perfect composure.

Not all the Jews were shot that night. Eighteen were left alive for the time being. They were ordered to fill the pit in with earth. They were on grave-digging duty. Twelve hours later, on the evening of 25 March, they themselves were murdered on the orders of Hans-Joachim Oldenburg, Margit's lover, and buried in a field near the abattoir.

After the war, seven people were prosecuted for committing multiple murder and atrocities, in other words crimes against humanity. They were Josef Muralter, Ludwig Groll, Stefan Beigelbeck, Eduard Nicka, Franz Podezin, Hildegard Stadler and Hans-Joachim Oldenburg. But in 1946 the trial ground to a halt, because the two principal witnesses were murdered. First of them was Karl Muhr, the ordnance officer at the castle. He had handed out the guns that night of 24 March, and saw the faces of those who would fire them later. A year later Muhr was found in the woods with a bullet in his head, his dead dog beside him, and his house was on fire. The cartridge case that the police took away from the crime scene disappeared. The second victim was Nikolaus Weiss, an eyewitness who had survived the massacre by hiding in a Rechnitz family's shed. A year later, when he was on his way to the town of Lockenhaus, someone shot at his car. It went into a skid, and Weiss died on the spot.

After these two murders, the people of Rechnitz lived in fear of retribution. No one talked. Their silence has lasted to this day. In the seventy years since the crime was committed, the town has become a symbol of Hungary under Austria, with its Nazi past. Any one who mentions Rechnitz is alluding to the suppression of facts.

On 15 July 1948, Stefan Beigelbeck and Hildegard Stadler were cleared. Ludwig Groll was condemned to eight years' imprisonment with hard labour, Josef Muralter was given five years and Eduard Nicka three years in prison. Podezin and Oldenburg, the ringleaders of the massacre, were on the run. The Burgenland police suspected that they were with Countess Margit Batthyány-Thyssen in Switzerland, living in an apartment not far from Lugano.

Interpol Vienna sent the Lugano police a telegram on 28 August 1948: 'Risk of the two men going to South America. Please arrest them.' The order to arrest the fugitives was posted in the Swiss Police Gazette, page 1643, on 30 August 1948, but there was no result.

Summing up at the end of the trial, Dr Mayer-Maly, the Austrian public prosecutor who was supposed to be clearing up the case of the massacre, said that 'The real murderers have not yet been found.'

*

I visited Rechnitz for the second time at the end of August, when the grapes were red and the trees in their full summer foliage. I had come to visit Annemarie Vitzthum, aged 89, and probably the last survivor of the guests at Margit's party.

'I'd really dolled myself up,' she remembered. 'We sat at round tables in the little hall on the ground floor, with the Count and Countess in the middle of the room. Countess Margit looked like a princess – she wore such lovely clothes.'

Men in uniform had kept coming and going, she told me, but she couldn't remember their names. 'There was such a commotion,' as she had also told the public prosecutor in 1947 when she was questioned. 'Everyone was drinking wine and dancing, except for me, I couldn't because I was only an ordinary girl, I was the telephonist.' At midnight a soldier had escorted her home, and up to that point the Countess had not left the castle. Frau Vitzthum had heard about the Jews only later, she said, as we ate her home-made sponge cake with crumble topping. What a terrible thing that was.

Then I went to see Klaus Gmeiner. He was Aunt Margit's forester, and had been the last person to see her alive. Margit owned 1000 hectares of land in Rechnitz, and came to hunt there every year. 'She was an excellent shot, she'd had experience of hunting game in Africa. She was very pleased when she bagged an animal, a mouflon or a deer, I never saw her happier.' In all the years since the war they had never mentioned the Nazi period, said Gmeiner, who like so many in Rechnitz thought Margit was wonderful. He was sure she had nothing to do with the crime, he told me.

'We went stalking,' he said of the evening before her death, 'and she hit a mouflon ram with a well-judged shot through the shoulder.' He remembered exactly how the animal had staggered twenty, maybe thirty steps towards her, and only then collapsed. He still recollected, he said, how she had complained that evening of all the people who kept begging her for money. 'That was the last thing she said.' Next morning she did not appear at breakfast time.

'How was it in Rechnitz? Did you find anything out?' my father asked me on the phone. He sounded tired. A few weeks earlier, a little dog had suddenly appeared outside the door of his weekend house on Lake Balaton, a mongrel who refused to move from his side.

'What's the dog doing?'

'Getting on my nerves.'

'But you like him, don't you?'

'Tell me about Rechnitz.'

'The people in the village called me Count, some of the women almost curtsied to me.'

'Terrible, all that fuss and bother.'

'Witnesses say Margit's husband was at the party too.'

'In the family it's always been claimed that he was in Hungary that evening.'

'Everyone tells a different version of the story: the family say they didn't know anything and never asked any questions about Margit's role; the media go to town with headlines about the blood-thirsty Countess; and the people of Rechnitz want to sweep the whole thing under the carpet. To them, Aunt Margit is a saint.'

'And what do you want?'

3

When I began investigating, I wanted to know what really happened. I searched archives, wrote letters, drew up files, and wondered who in our family knew anything about Rechnitz, and why no one talked about it. I had often heard my grandparents discussing aunts long dead, the quirks of some uncle or other, the former splendour of Hungary, when people still knew how to behave and had good taste. Why did I never hear a word about Rechnitz? Why no mention of that mass grave? I thought I might find a clue in the place where the 180 bodies were buried. It's possible someone there might talk to you, I told myself, because you're one of the family.

But then, one winter evening, a chance meeting had many consequences. I was out and about in the city with friends, and in a restaurant we met an acquaintance sharing a table with the German writer Maxim Biller. We joined them, and at some point the conversation came around to Aunt Margit. Biller had heard of her, which surprised me, and he was the first person ever to ask me, 'And what's that to do with you?'

The Nazi Countess, as the papers call her to this day, and me?

I hadn't expected such a question. Absurd as it may sound, I had never yet put it to myself. Strictly speaking, I told Biller awkwardly, we weren't even related; Margit was a Thyssen who had married into our family. 'So what's that to do with me?' I repeated, playing for time. 'Nothing, why would it? It's all so long ago.'

If he were to ask me the same question today, I would have a different answer. Because my focus changed over the course of time. It became less and less a matter of finding out what really happened; I was no longer a journalist approaching the subject from outside, making notes, gathering facts and asking other people questions. Now it was all about me.

I read about associations of grandchildren affected by the war, people of my own age who, because of events seventy years in the past, feel uprooted, disorientated, as if they had been born in a vacuum. 'They have inherited their parents' unresolved emotions,' I read, 'and now they are trying to break free of the fetters of the past.' Many would feel guilty for being unable to mitigate their parents' distress and confusion. I read about some who were too hard on themselves, about the deliberate construction of ideal worlds to compensate for a sense of something lacking. One man wrote, 'I want to arrive in my own life at last.' Another asked, 'What kind of people has our parents' persistent silence made us?' I recognized myself in such remarks, although I didn't want to belong to a community of suffering. I am not the type to join self-help groups.

'Every generation has its own tasks,' said a website dealing with the subject. 'The parental generation rolled up their sleeves and set to work clearing up the outer rubble. Clearing up the inner rubble is the grandchildren's task.' Is that so? Wasn't it too simple? I had already read that trauma can be inherited, and indeed is particularly likely to be passed on from grandparents to their grandchildren, but I didn't entirely believe it. As if the hail of bombs through which my father lived as a child was an excuse for my occasional melancholy. As if the ten years my grandfather spent in the gulag in Siberia accounted for my eccentricity. And yet there was a connection – or did I just imagine it?

Wasn't I the one who always felt guilty for being too comfortably off in Switzerland? Didn't I sometimes, secretly, wish for a small-scale war? Or at least a crisis. And think how often, as a journalist, I had written about migrants. I accompanied one family on their journey out of Iraq; I spent several days with Africans working in the hothouses of southern Spain; and with refugees from Bangladesh in old warehouses in Athens. Why did I take such an interest in fugitives? Where did my attraction to suffering come from?

You grew up in Zürich, I told myself, far from armoured mortar-throwers, what's the matter with you? You dried plants at school, marsh marigolds, blackthorn blossom, your teacher was proud of your herbarium. And then there was that backhand you hit in the third set in 1988, a one-handed shot winning the match and getting you out of trouble, your socks red with the sand of the tennis court, that's your life, isn't it good enough for you? No, it never was. There was always something missing. The cloudless world around me, as white as the polo shirts I wore, turning up their collars in the mid-eighties, was never mine. And the longer I thought about it, the more accurate it seemed to say: I am a grandchild of the war. My father spent the war in an air-raid shelter, my grandfather was dragged off to Siberia by the Russians, my grandmother lost her second son – and my great-aunt was responsible for the massacre of 180 Jews. They were perpetrators and victims, hunted and hunters, were first acclaimed and then despised: the bastards of international history. In the end they went through life with their backs increasingly bent, losing first their self-respect and then their voices. *We were a family of moles*, wrote my grandmother Maritta in her diary. *We withdrew, we did not believe in anything any more, we retreated into ourselves, keeping our heads down underground, always ducking.*

And how about me?

4

I remembered one of my last visits to my grandmother in Budapest. It must have been in 2006, before I knew anything about Rechnitz. In her last years, my grandmother was obsessed by the idea of writing the story of her life. At first she tried using a typewriter, an old 1970s model with a coloured ribbon. But she soon found typing too much of a strain, and went on writing by hand, in a script dating from a time when horse-drawn coaches still drove along the streets. 'How are your memoirs getting on?' I asked, but she was already on her feet, setting off for the kitchen at the end of the long corridor to make tea. I heard her searching the cutlery drawer for teaspoons.

'Are they in separate chapters?' I called after her, without expecting an answer. Not that I was eager to read her notes at the time; it was a polite question, because we didn't have much else in common to talk about. I was only trying to bridge the awkward silence that always fell when we saw each other.

She took milk out of the fridge, poured it into a small jug, and as she did so she must have spilt some of it. '*Nem jó,*' she exclaimed: not good. I heard her slapping her thigh with the palm of her hand in annoyance as she mopped up the milk on the floor and wrung out the dishcloth. The kettle was whistling. Photographs of family members whose names I could never remember stood on the low bookshelves. I always had to bend down to look, stooping until I was bowing low to them. Who knows, maybe that was the idea. Yellowed engravings showing scenes of Hungary before the

First World War hung on the walls: images of the old Austro-Hungarian Empire. My father and grandmother had talked of nothing else since my childhood, and I used to nod politely, but I was never really interested. And if I did happen to ask a question, for instance what it had been like to go hunting in those days, or why Hungary was so anti-Semitic, as everyone claimed in recent years, I always got the same answer. *'Nem érted'* [you don't understand]. I grew up with that remark ringing in my ears, and it haunts me to this day.

And: 'You don't understand,' I also hear the dead men in the photo frames calling as I pass them, bowing low.

'But I've read about it. What more do you want?' I call back.

'None of that's worth anything,' they reply. 'Forget it,' they add in chorus.

'I . . .'

'Have you ever had to suffer?'

'Suffer?'

'Do you know what ivories are?'

'Ivories?'*

'Have you ever lost your house, your native place, your country?'

'But . . .'

'No buts,' they interrupt me in the tones of Imperial-and-Royal Austro-Hungarian army officers. 'You just don't understand.'

'What were we talking about?' my grandmother asked. She had come back from the kitchen with a tea tray, two white cups with curved handles, a sugar container with the corners knocked off, and a small jug of milk. I hadn't noticed her coming; my nose was pressed to the cold living-room window, where I stood watching the entrance to the palace on Castle Hill, Hungarian flags blowing in the

---

* Translator's note: in German, *Grandeln*, a hunting term for the canine teeth of deer, taken as trophies to be worn, for instance, in cufflinks.

wind, and a violinist in Baroque costume with a wig, bowing whenever a tourist put a couple of forints into his collecting box.

'I was asking whether any of your memoirs are ready to be seen yet,' I replied. She smiled and waved the question away.

'How was your journey?' she asked.

These visits lasted three days. We would sit on the blue sofa in my grandmother's overheated living room, and time dragged. We passed the hours by keeping our trickle of conversation going, up until supper on the last day. 'What good soup,' I said, sounding to myself like a senior citizen on Austrian television. 'It's home-made,' she told me, and her remark suited her no better than mine had suited me. It was as if we were actors playing the parts of grandma and grandson. And hadn't our walks on the previous days, collecting chestnuts, had something of a stage set about them too, as we very cautiously moved from subject to subject, touching on them only very lightly, as if we were walking through a minefield?

When we said goodbye she always held me for a moment longer in her arms. '*Nagyon szeretlek,*' she whispered in my ear, 'I love you very much.' Upon which I hugged her bony shoulders in a similarly conspiratorial way. Were we doing something forbidden?

I saw my grandmother for the last time in a hospital somewhere in Budapest city centre, one of those huge buildings with a sooty façade that doesn't tell you, from the outside, whether it is an opera house, a prison, or as in this case a hospital. She was thin, and looked lost in her bed. I went to a little kiosk round the corner to buy her yoghurt, Red Bull, biscuits and chocolate, because my father had said the hospital food was terrible and she needed to build up her strength. When I came back with these items, their wrapping colourfully printed with words like 'energy' and 'power' that had nothing to do with her, she looked at me in alarm and shook her head. She couldn't go on any longer.

On her deathbed, she begged my father in a faint voice to promise that the notes she had been writing would be burnt. It was her last wish, and he held her hand, but he didn't keep his word. She died on 1 May 2009, on a cold, icy morning. I was in a café in Zürich, watching several water cannon being moved into position outside ready for demonstrators – that happened every year on Labour Day – when I got a text message from my father. Only a line to say that she had died in the night. I paid my bill, left the café, and walked past young people in Palestinian headdresses, holding banners and denouncing the banks, past Kurdish activists, Tibetans, feminists and bawling teenagers in hoodies, I opened the door of our apartment and took my daughter, three months old at the time, out of her cradle. 'Your great-granny is dead,' I whispered. She was holding her little fists in front of her eyes in her sleep, and I regretted what I had said as soon as the words were out of my mouth.

Instead of destroying the diary, my father stuffed the sheets of paper into a dull green folder, added more letters and notes that he had found in one of the lower drawers of my grandmother's desk, put it all into a shopping bag and stowed it away in a cupboard in his own apartment. He didn't read a line of it. Not a word. He knew that he hadn't fulfilled her last wish, and didn't want to let his mind dwell on it. When he gave me the bag two years after her death, he didn't say much. We were sitting at a corner table in Da Lello, his favourite Italian restaurant on Márvány Utca in Budapest, when, without a word, he handed me all that was left of his mother.

Diaries I

Maritta

Everyone was nervous all day long. Goga, Sophie, and the rest of the household staff and the ladies' maids kept hurrying up and down the corridors with clean cloths, boiled water, fruit. The dogs howled. No one actually mentioned the word 'birth', everyone used the more elegant French term, *l'événement*, 'the event', which didn't in the least suit this place, Sárosd, a Hungarian village surrounded by marshy land on the outermost rim of Western Europe, a place where there was nothing but a few farmers cultivating their fields with donkeys; gypsy girls who were always pregnant and whose children sometimes froze to death in winter; and a castle with thick, yellow walls, with little turrets and gables, where my parents and my elder sister lived. Even Peti and Zoli, the old coachman and the saddler with his stiff left leg, spoke of *levenma*, pronouncing the last syllable with a deep 'a' sound, just as when they were hunting they called *tiro!* and *obak!* Instead of *tire haut!* and *au bas!* They brought out the old armoured mortar that had been forgotten in the vineyards after the First World War, hitched it to the horses and pushed it into the inner courtyard, where it left deep ruts in the gravel on the ground. On that sultry day, 30 June 1922, it was to be fired to drive away the storm clouds. At seven-thirty in the evening, the moment came. Five deafening shots rose to the sky. And I came into the world, to be dressed in the finest batiste.

Agnes

My name is Agnes, but everyone calls me Agi. I was born in Sárosd, a small village in Hungary where exactly six Jewish families lived. We were one of them. I had a brother two years younger than me, named Sándor; my father was called Imre, my mother was Gitta. We were what you would think of as a normal family. Today we would be described as middle class, neither rich nor poor. We had a German nanny, so I spoke a little German. I went to elementary school in the village. Later, my parents sent me to boarding-school in Budapest, where I felt lonely, cried every day, and was homesick for my old life. I began to get used to the boarding-school only gradually, after about a year, and when I was fourteen my parents rented a room for me in a family's house.

My brother Sándor was living in Budapest too, but we didn't often see each other. In the morning we went to school, in the afternoon we studied or worked. At the same time I was taking a training course at the well-known confectioner's shop, Ruszwurm in the Castle district. My parents thought there might be hard times coming for us, and it would be a good thing if I was trained to follow some useful trade. In the worst case, they thought, I would have to emigrate to Australia, because we had a woman cousin there. But I didn't want to think about all that. What could happen to me?

Maritta

When my father saw me, he nodded and smiled, shook hands, looked briefly into the bedroom and saw the bloodstains on the bed, and his wife being tended, looked at the wall, where an old engraving hung. It showed Jesus on the Cross, with shoulder-length hair and a suffering expression on his face.

I never heard a cross word spoken, yet it was obvious that my parents had wanted nothing more fervently than a boy. An heir. Women were worth nothing in Hungary at the time, and I venture to doubt whether it's any different today. But of course I had a privileged life. I drank milk from a cow specially chosen for me, unlike the other village children I had shoes to wear in the hard winters, white frilly dresses in summer, a chambermaid to look after my room, cooks, and a French tutor called Louis, who also taught me good manners.

But to be privileged doesn't mean being spoilt; one shouldn't confuse the two. Not like today, when well-to-do parents give their children whatever they want, however far-fetched. We weren't allowed to express a wish for anything, we weren't allowed to complain; one doesn't weep and wail, we were always told, that was one of the most important commandments: we must keep our composure. The nursery that my sister and I occupied was furnished in a very Spartan style, with few toys, hardly any heating, and we were given sweets only on special occasions. Pocket money in the form of cash was something that I scarcely knew about in my childhood; there was something forbidden, even vulgar about it. Instead, there was a timetable to be rigidly observed: eating, praying, reading. Our privileged life meant that more was expected of us than of the less privileged. And above all, we must never show off; that was another commandment. We must always be modest, and never boast of doing something particularly well.

Two years before my birth, on 4 June 1920, Hungary had signed the Trianon peace treaty. To this day it is regarded as the greatest disaster in the history of the country. Hungary lost more than two-thirds of its former territory. After the First World War, the Allied powers divided the country up among the neighbouring states: Romania got Transylvania, 63,000 square kilometres of land went to Czechoslovakia, what is now Vojvodina went to the new kingdom of the Serbs, Croats and Slovenians, and Austria acquired the Burgenland. Hungary, once so powerful, became a dwarf state.

The Trianon treaty was a shock to the whole country. Friends and relations of mine still remember that dark day, describing their pain as if they had lost their arms and legs when the treaty was signed near Paris.

Even in the 1930s, every school day began with a prayer for the restoration of Greater Hungary: 'I believe in one God, I believe in one homeland, I believe in the infinite truth of God, I believe in the resurrection of Hungary.'

And I vividly remember the rage that we all felt within ourselves. The whole country was crying out, but made no sound. The mutilation of our native land had made me and my countrymen into fanatical Hungarians: we were obsessed by the idea of liberty, sad at heart and deeply defiant.

Like so many other families, we had a little plaque on our house showing a map. In the background, you could see the delicate outlines of the former kingdom, from Cracow to Trieste, from the southern Tyrol to Belgrade, and in the middle, like a wound, the misshapen thing that it had become now. 'Can this go on?' asked wording under the map, and with it the answer: '*Nem! Nem! Soha!*' No, no, never!

While democratic structures developed in large parts of Europe between the wars, Hungary remained a backward country. It was a semi-feudal corporate state in which society was organized in social classes, each of which had its own obligations. Apart from an intellectual, cultural and scientific elite in Budapest, predominantly Jewish, Hungarian society was made up of the aristocratic owners of landed estates, which included my family, and hundreds of thousands of agricultural labourers.

This was the time of Admiral Miklós Horthy, Regent of Hungary. Horthy took office riding a white horse, like our legendary hero of the past Prince Árpád. Modern historians dispute how far Horthy was anti-Semitic in making it difficult for Jews to study, even before race laws were introduced into Germany. He fought side by side with Hitler for a long time, and did not really dis-associate himself from the Führer until the second half of the year 1944. It must be remembered that, to his credit, in the end he tried to stop deportation trains leaving for Auschwitz. One train did stop at the border, obeying Horthy's orders, and even came back, but against Eichmann, who was in Budapest at the time, he was power-less and could not save the Jews any more. I can say of Horthy only that I think of the 24 years of his regency with respect and gratitude. My happy childhood and unsuspecting youth fell into that span of time.

People of my parents' generation were feudal through and through. You have to imagine their life in the country at the time as something like the films about American cotton plantations in the Deep South: the estate owners on one side, their slaves on the other. Those who were lucky found work with a right-minded family. But many who were not so lucky were treated like dogs. My father was stern with his labourers, but always just. A patriarch. Every morning we had to eat breakfast with him at a long table. He insisted on hair that had been brushed and combed, and neatly ironed blouses. The portraits of our ancestors hung on the walls, men with military dec-orations, women in draped dresses, and there were great pairs of antlers over the doorways. Every day we had a cup of malt coffee, but we children hated the brew because it tasted so bitter. True, there were always two sugar lumps on my saucer, but I wasn't allowed to dissolve them in the coffee, as a reminder not to indulge myself. I had to put them back in a bowl that stood in the middle of the table and had the words *Pour les Pauvres* engraved on its lid. I don't know where that sugar bowl is today, and I don't know where it came from, I only know that it was part of my youth, like my teacher's cane. When the bowl was full, we were told, the sugar lumps would be given to the poor in the village, but I saw them being used instead to sugar the sweet bread that we offered to guests in the drawing-room. These days, children would challenge their parents for that deceit and tell them how underhand their conduct was, how hypocritical they were. But we held our tongues.

The castle where we lived wasn't to be called a castle because there was something vulgar about that word, too. We spoke of the estate. The house was in a U shape round a gravel courtyard with a chestnut tree in the middle of it, and the tree was surrounded by a bench. There were at least thirty rooms, and wooden trellises on the south wall going up to the windows, with climbing roses growing on them, red, green and white, the colours of the Hungarian flag. The scent of roses hung in the air for half the year, and when it was suddenly gone, when you smelled the marsh instead of roses, wet earth and rotting vegetation, you knew that autumn had come.

Agnes

Everything went on as usual until 19 March 1944. It was a Sunday. A girlfriend phoned and asked me, 'Have you heard? The Germans have captured Budapest.' But I couldn't believe it, because there was no sign of any such thing in the streets. That Sunday I had lunch with a man I knew, and then went to the cinema with my brother, which was unusual. We didn't do many things together, but that particular day he had said, 'If you're not doing anything else, let's go and see a film.' We were sitting in the auditorium, the film had been running for some time when the light suddenly went on, and we were told to leave the cinema. The management said they were very sorry, but the show was over because the Germans had marched in. Incredulously, we stood up and went out into the street. My way home was past a large building where the pro-Nazi Hungarian Arrow Cross Party had its office. I had never liked passing it, but I liked it less than ever that day. The men in their black shirts standing outside the building and talking to each other scared me.

My father had been coming to Budapest the following morning

31

to do some business, but I phoned and told him to stay at home. I didn't think the situation could be dangerous, I said, but I thought it would be safer to stay away. Maybe the Germans would bomb the railway tracks. They had done that in other parts of Hungary.

'But why don't you want me to come?' asked my father. So the news hadn't reached the village yet.

'It's better that way,' I said, untruthfully. I didn't want him to worry unnecessarily about me and my brother. But my voice must have given me away, because he sensed my alarm. I can still remember the last thing he said. 'And what will become of you two?'

Maritta

I was sixteen, and had one thing above all others in my head – my books. I didn't care about politics, and my life was still a matter of everyday concerns, even when Austria was annexed by the Germans in 1938. So far, however, no one in Hungary saw that as a danger. I read and read, for nights on end, and I wrote terrible poems about homesickness. I had no idea of love, and it was never mentioned in the convent of the Sacré-Cœur nuns, where I spent my last three years of middle school. Early in my life I decided to put the subject of men last. My mother was so beautiful and my sister so popular that I voluntarily took a back seat, and just looked at men on the sly. But because it was the thing to do, I too had to introduce possible candidates for marriage to my parents, which was a difficulty, because there really wasn't anyone. Until I met a young man at a ball, and oddly enough he said from the first that he loved me. He was to keep his promise to love me always for the rest of his life. Feri was the only man in my life; our marriage lasted until his death. It was a remarkable relationship.

At the time you talked of someone's 'financial background'. That didn't mean how much money he had; more important were his education, his culture, his appearance and conduct, and a certain manner of speech. A single word could betray someone's social class and origin. What made him a man was what mattered, not what he owned. Feri seemed to be a suitable husband for me, or so at least everyone said. He was a Batthyány, I was an Esterházy; we both came from great Hungarian families. I didn't pay much attention to all that talk; I liked my books better. But if getting married meant I would have more time for reading afterwards, I was happy with that. So directly after our wedding in February 1942, we moved to Budapest, and very soon I was pregnant. Feri was called up, and went to Poland and the front there. I felt very much alone in Budapest, so in the summer I moved home to Sárosd again with my baby son.

I remember that journey home as if it were yesterday. Even on the short railway trip, as I heard the rhythm of the wheels, watching the telegraph poles rise and fall as we passed them, my anxiety for my husband, fighting somewhere in Poland, faded. It was blurred by the fields, meadows, the lines of poplar trees and elder bushes. Cranes danced on the horizon. Then the name of the village was called, the train stopped, the notices on the station disappeared behind sooty steam that quickly dispersed again, showing me Peti the coachman waiting for me at the very end of the platform. He was wearing bustard's feathers in his hat, he raised his hand – and with his greeting all the familiarity of my childhood was back again.

I had been away from Feri for a year now, getting his letters from the front; he was in Poland, and later in the Ukraine. Poor dear, he wouldn't have hurt a fly. Feri was an anxious man, and those who knew him well said he was as naïve and good-natured as a child – and so he was. In his letters he spoke of his love for me, and his longing to begin a real life with me at last. I missed him, too, although I couldn't claim that my heart was burning for him.

Agnes

That day, March the 19th at eleven p.m., the phone rang for me. It was my father, telling me to come home by the first train tomorrow morning. By now, I assumed, news of the Germans had reached our village. My brother didn't want to go back. He thought it might be better for us to stay in Budapest, rather than going to Sárosd, where everyone knew us. Budapest was a big city, he said, we could hide there.

'I'll go anyway,' I said. 'But I'll come back, with Mother and Father.'

'Do that.' He went to the station with me, to help me with my suitcase.

There were German soldiers, with their dogs, standing in all the big squares. Hungarian police officers were checking the trams. The door of ours opened, they came in and ordered all Jews to get out. A police officer told me, 'Young woman, if you're not Jewish you'd better run away.' I said, 'What about my brother?'

'He must get out.'

'Then I'm getting out, too.'

And so we were taken to the worst prison of the time in Hungary, in Kistarcsa, not far from Budapest. It was cold, with snow lying on the roads, on the trees, on the rooftops of the houses. What must it have been like for my parents, standing on the station at home and waiting for us, when we never got off the train? To this day I can't imagine it, the pain is too great.

They separated us outside the prison. We women were taken into a small room with no windows; they left the men in the yard.

I had an apple in my pocket, and I broke it in half with my fingers, meaning to give Sándor one of the halves as soon as I saw him again. But he didn't show up.

A few days later it was the Jewish festival of Pesach. We were given soup brought in by Jewish organizations. I remember that we had no plates and no spoons, but we were so hungry that we couldn't wait for it to cool down. Some of us tried eating soup with their bare hands, and burnt themselves. I had a powder compact with me, and filled it with soup, using the compact as a bowl. It was as tiny as if I were a doll.

Maritta

Soon after my return to Sárosd, I noticed how much the house had changed, and after a while German soldiers billeted themselves on us too. They had taken over a few rooms, their cars stood by our beloved chestnut tree with the bench around it. By now the last of the men who could have helped on the home farm had disappeared. Most of them had been called up and gone to fight on the front, where they were wounded or deserted. The saddler had gone, and so had the stable boy, the gardener, and his son. The lawn was running wild, the roses withered. No one tended the cattle, carp died in the fish ponds, and the fields lay fallow. My father asked the Germans if they would let him put the village Jews to work for us, and they did. From that day on, about twenty Jews came to the farm every morning. They wore yellow stars on their jackets. The Goldner brothers helped with the horses, the Medaks and the Mandls worked in the garden, the rest went out to the fields. We knew many of them, we wished them good day, and they greeted us back. But those who didn't know us were too frightened to look us in the eyes – what had we done? We were friends with the Mandls in particular. They had a delicatessen shop, and ran the only petrol station in the neighbourhood, and when we were children they always used to slip sweets into our pockets. The Mandls, a married couple, had two children of my age, Agi and Sándor, and we had always played together in the past.

The most obvious sign that there was war in Europe again was the fact that fewer and fewer huntsmen came visiting. They had been sent to the front. Germans and Hungarians fought side by side, and hunting society thinned out like my uncles' hair. Conversations were quieter, jokes were few and far between. Rum stayed where it was, in bottles. The huntsmen were fighting with Hitler in the Ukraine, shooting human beings and not hares these days.

5

A few months after that evening with Maxim Biller, I lay down on Daniel Strassberg's couch for the first time. I knew that his mother had survived the Holocaust, and that after the war his father had smuggled Jews over the Swiss border to Marseilles. They went on from that seaport to Palestine; the state of Israel did not exist yet. When I read that he had done research into how far family histories are inherited, I knew he was the right psychoanalyst for me. This was an experiment, I told him on that first visit to his consulting room near the University. The sight of his cream couch in the middle of the room reminded me of an operating table, and I noticed the books on the shelves – Freud, Lacan – and the pleasant aroma in the air of thousands upon thousands of pipes that he had smoked here. 'I want to know what's still left in my bones from earlier times,' I told him. 'I'd like to find out what influence past events have in making us what we are.'

'We can try,' he said, but I was to forget the experiment idea, he added, and I should never prepare in advance for a session. 'It's not supposed to degenerate into a game,' he said, and I nodded, although I was not entirely sure what he meant, and had no idea what would come of it. From then on I lay on his couch twice a week, staring at the ceiling. On Wednesdays and Fridays my clothes always smelt of cold smoke.

Every session began with the same rituals. I sat in his waiting-room, leafing through old magazines. When I heard him opening his door and coming along the corridor, I stood up and almost furtively offered him my hand, although he knew me better than most of my friends did, and I saw him more often than I saw my parents. But there was something secret about our proximity. We couldn't clap one another on the back on meeting after we hadn't seen each other for a few days. I couldn't thank him at the end of a session, although I had wanted to do so several times. As soon as I left that couch our intimacy was gone, and we were strangers in the real world: if we were to meet by chance looking at the cheese display in the supermarket, I wouldn't know what to talk to him about – Gorgonzola? It would feel like a betrayal. As if two people who met secretly in hotel rooms, always in the evening, were suddenly to encounter each other at seven in the morning, in the glaring neon lighting of the underground station, and feel alarmed at the sight.

Before lying down I adjusted the wine-red cushion that still showed the imprint of my predecessor's head, while Strassberg sat down in his chair behind me. The first few minutes were usually tough going. I rubbed my eyes, adjusted my sweater, and sensed him watching me – watching me doing what? What made me so sure of that? Maybe he was checking the length of his fingernails, maybe he was taking a last look at his telephone; I didn't know what he was doing while I told him all about my life. I looked up at the ceiling, from there my eyes wandered to the books, I smelled the pipe tobacco in the air, closed my eyes so as to concentrate. Outside, the trams drove by, the number 7 and the number 13, on which I always used to ride home to the little house on the outskirts of the city in my youth. I took the number 13 to the terminus, and from there I boarded a bus that took me past fields yellow with oilseed rape in summer, white with snow in winter. Then it was another few minutes on foot to our front door, which my mother had had painted green before we moved in. She had also had a heavy brass doorknob fitted; no one else in the street had one like it, only us. Our door would have been right for a house in the countryside of eastern Europe, or maybe in rainy England, somewhere on a hill in Devon, but not for our little 1970s house in the suburbs of Zürich. It was the wrong door in the wrong house; I told Strassberg all that without stopping to think. The words came out of my mouth, light as feathers; I felt like one of those birds that swoop above the water of a lake, only occasionally touching the surface – the smell of pipe smoke was gone, the books, the cracks in the ceiling. And there were no trams outside. Such moments, moments when I forgot everything around me, occurred in almost every session. Until something brought me back to earth, a sound, a thought, until the shapes of the bookshelves stood out on the wall again, the noise of traffic in the street came into the room. I had just been swooping over the water, and now I was standing up to my neck in it.

Strassberg said nothing.

'But none of that matters,' I said, trying to return to that hovering condition, just as you try to turn over and go back to sleep in the morning, or in the evening you drink another glass of wine hoping to prolong the effect of the three before it, but did that ever happen?

'Did you see that film made in the eighties, *Back to the Future*?' I asked him. 'There's a boy in it who flies back to the past in a car.'

'Yes, I've seen it.'

'He has a photo from the present with him as he goes back in time. It shows him, his parents, and his brother and sister. But the children in the picture visibly fade away, because theoretically speaking they can't exist yet, and his parents haven't even met.'

'I remember that.'

'That's how I've always felt, like the children in that picture: as if I were only half here, getting more and more transparent. Does that make sense?'

'Why not?'

'As if I were disappearing. Running over the snow and leaving no trace.'

Silence.

'But when I went to Rechnitz, and began asking my father all those questions, that sense of disappearance suddenly went away. Maybe that's why I came to consult you.'

'I don't understand that part of it.'

'So as to exist.'

Strassberg didn't say a word. I waited, but there was no answer.

'I sound worse than a women's magazine, don't I?'

Then he took a deep breath and held it, as he always did at the end of a session. 'I'm afraid our time is up,' he said, in a rather strained voice, and let the air out again as if he didn't like interrupting things at this point, which I could well understand. We shook hands again on parting, as quickly as possible.

Diaries II

Maritta

It's late in the afternoon. I am lying on the bed in my room, reading. What book? Heavens, I can't remember. Maybe *War and Peace*? Yes, that could have been it. Tolstoy. A shout tears me away from my reading; I put the book down, stand up and look out of the window. My son is asleep in his little bed beside me, my second child is still inside me.

The gravel in the courtyard is churned up, I can see the tracks of tyres, there are no leaves on the ground – naturally, since it is early summer. Every room in our house is full of soldiers, refugees, wounded men. The dogs are extremely agitated, Mother has been in a sanatorium for weeks. From my window I can see my father. He is standing on the drive with Herr Mandl opposite him, waving his arms. Herr Mandl is wearing a light-coloured raincoat much too large for him. I go downstairs and out into the courtyard, with gravel crunching under my feet. Herr Mandl looks me in the eyes; my father does not turn round.

'They're on the way to a concentration camp, they'll die,' says Herr Mandl. He means Agnes and Sándor, the Mandls' children. It seems that they are already on one of the trains. Frau Mandl is clutching her rake and shouting at my father as I have never heard anyone shout at him before. 'Help us! Help us, do something!' But my father does nothing. Then I hear two shots being fired.

And what do I do? I run to the village church to make my

confession, and as I am about to sit in the confessional I fall down in a faint. 'It's the agitation,' says our village priest, but I know he is wrong. I feel very cold. I remember that extremely well. I have felt the cold all my life, even in summer, but I will never forget the icy cold of that confessional. And when I come back to my senses, I have only one thought in my mind: I could at least have saved the Mandls. At least them.

6

On a misty, damp November day in 1956 my grandmother, her husband Feri, who had come back from the gulag only a year earlier, and my father, fourteen years old at the time, fled from Hungary. Soviet tanks had been rattling through Budapest for a week. About 10,000 freedom fighters faced the Soviets, most of them students. Many Hungarians left their country at that time, going across the fields by night to avoid the soldiers, swimming rivers, climbing barbed wire fences. My grandparents and my father took a taxi to the Austro-Hungarian border and simply strolled under the barriers as if they were out for a Sunday walk. As my grandfather also had an Austrian passport, there was no difficulty about crossing the border. He was carrying two suitcases and holding my father's hand. 'I have seen dead horses in the streets of Budapest since I was a child,' was the way my father began his account of the flight. From Austria they went on into Switzerland, to Aunt Margit and Uncle Ivan, who took them in at their villa, the Villa Mita, in Lugano at the foot of Monte Brè. 'I remember the chauffeur who met us at the station,' said my father. 'Then I was taken to my room because I had a temperature. Next morning I wake up, the sun is shining directly on the bed, there are palm trees in the garden. My uncle Ivan comes in and asks if I would like to go for a spin in the Ferrari, and I ask myself: am I in Heaven?'

There are few family documents from that time on the banks of Lake Lugano, only a few letters from my grandmother to a cousin in Vienna, complaining to her, if one reads between the lines, because she can't stand it there, she hates staying with Ivan and Margit. 'Even Paradise has its drawbacks,' she writes, refraining from putting it more clearly. She mustn't complain; that was drummed into her in her childhood.

The Villa Mita lies right on the banks of Lake Lugano. From its living-room, you can see Italy on the other side of the lake, and on fine days you can make out the church towers of little villages, but not on winter evenings in the middle of February in 1957, or so I imagine it, anyway – the clouds hanging low, the wind roughening the surface of the water, pale rugs on the living-room floor, soft leather sofas, stags' antlers hanging on the walls, and something else exotic. Ivory, perhaps? The skin of an antelope? After all, both Margit and Ivan had often been on safari to Africa since moving from Rechnitz to Lugano in 1945.

What will those evenings have been like? 'Time for a sherry,' Ivan could have said, being a good-tempered man who always felt he had to keep everyone happy. Ivan is tall, wears beige trousers and a shirt of the same colour, with a blue signet ring on his finger and a gold Dupont lighter in his pocket. 'I'd rather have a beer,' my grandfather Feri, Ivan's younger brother, may have replied. As I imagine it, he is sitting near the fireplace looking down at his shoes, seeing a strip of pale, hairless calf between his socks and his trousers. He would have felt comfortable beside the fire, enjoying the warmth. He lost one of his little toes in the camps of Western Siberia where he spent ten years.

My grandmother sits at the window, smoking and reading the newspaper. She can't stand Ivan's good humour, and rolls her eyes. For the first few weeks since their arrival in Lugano she tried to suppress her discomfort, but now she can do it no longer. *Don't you see that people are dying?* she may have been thinking in the silence. She looks back at the front page of the *Neue Zürcher Zeitung*. On that day the trials of those involved in the popular rising in Hungary are beginning. Eleven people are sitting on the defendants' bench. 'The principal defendant,' she reads, 'is 25-year-old medical student Ilona Tóth.' She grinds out her cigarette, blows her nose on the tissue that was tucked up the sleeve of her sweater, tears a corner off the tissue, rolls it into a tiny pellet and puts it in her mouth. What times are we living in, she wonders, when people fighting for freedom are prosecuted? And she shakes her head.* 'The lie has gained credence,' she writes in her letter to her cousin. 200,000 refugees, 2,500 dead, those are the figures that weigh on her mind. Weeks after the Soviet army marched into Budapest, the failure of the Hungarian uprising is still on the front page. Don't you mind about that? she would have liked to shout, but the words stick in her throat. She lights herself another cigarette. Somehow or other she must hold on.

'What would you like to drink, my dear?' asks Ivan, catching her eye. He has just been telling them how wonderful it will be here in May, when you can go straight from the living-room and into the lake. 'Marvellous, I tell you, simply marvellous.'

'A glass of wine would be nice.' She smiles at him. She would sooner die than stay here until May.

She should really be happy. Her husband is back from captivity, they are together in freedom for the first time since their wedding fifteen years ago. Her son is well, and has an opportunity of getting to know his father at last. So what, she will have wondered, is the matter? She looks out at the bare branches of the trees, the cold grass in the garden, the waves breaking on the shore. It is the weight of past years on her shoulders, as so often. 'Cold inside,' is what she calls it, she has already written about it. But like everything that she writes – poems, short stories – she throws it on the fire.

Ivan brings her the wine and puts the glass down on a mahogany coaster with a horse motif on it. He gave it to Margit for Christmas. He talks about good vintages, but my grandmother will

* Author's note: Ilona Tóth was falsely accused of murdering a member of the Hungarian Security Police. She died on the gallows in 1957, at the age of 25.

not have been listening. She would rather be back in bed with her books, under the covers with her great love, Thomas Mann.

At six-thirty Margit comes down the stairs. In my imagination, she glances at herself briefly in the mirror before entering the drawing-room, aware that at that moment everyone will stop talking. And so they do that evening, as usual. Feri claps his hands – 'There she is.' He speaks German with an Austrian accent. 'You look enchanting,' says Ivan.

'Oh, never mind all that nonsense,' she says, dismissing the compliment, although she certainly thinks that he is right. She is wearing her soft tweed Chanel suit, just right for the weather, emphasizing her legs and slimming her behind, as she likes. But her guests probably haven't heard of Coco Chanel. She would rather be in good company in the Ritz in Paris than here, surrounded by these Hungarian refugees.

'Well, how are you today, my dear?' she says to my grand-mother in a tone of too much pity, I imagine. Slightly mocking, as nurses talk to their patients.

Or no, wait, it wasn't like that. Margit comes downstairs, thinks of Paris and the Ritz, goes over to the window and tries to strike as neutral a note as possible. 'Well, how are you today, my dear?' It is my grandmother who will have picked up the touch of condescension in that remark. Yes, it could have been like that.

'I told Jóska that we'd eat at seven,' says Margit. 'What are you drinking? Ivan, would you be kind enough to bring me a sherry too?' Ivan goes into the dining-room. The fire can be heard crack-ling, and Ivan takes the cork out of a bottle. He comes back and pours himself more sherry as well. They all raise their glasses to each other.

'What filthy weather,' says Margit in her nasal voice, putting out her tongue barely perceptibly.

'I was just telling them how lovely it is here in May,' says Ivan.

'What's the temperature outside now?' asks Feri. 'I'm sure it can't be under three degrees, or we'd smell it in the air. There won't be snow tonight.'*

The clock strikes seven, they all get up, go into the next room, and sit down at the dinner table.

* Author's note: After prison camp, my grandfather was positively obsessed with the weather, and above all the temperature. In the camp, the weather had often been the only subject of conversation, as Varlam Shalamov wrote in his books about life in the gulag. To his death, my grandfather checked on the temperature out of doors several times a day.

IVAN   My grandfather's elder brother. He is 46 years old in 1957. His hair is elegantly swept back. Ivan likes fast cars and expensive suits, particularly in dark blue, and he cannot resist young women. He is well known as a good conversationalist, like many Hungarians he tends to exaggerate, and he will do anything to get in a good punch line. He has never done a day's work in his life, he speaks four languages fluently, and travels a great deal, mainly to Vienna where everyone addresses him, respectfully, as Count. He has often been to Africa to hunt big game. He bought a *hacienda* of 2,800 hectares in Uruguay with his wife's money, and Uruguayan citizenship to go with it. Ivan is a member of the Lugano Golf Club, and of the exclusive Corviglia Ski Club in St. Moritz.

AUNT MARGIT   One of the richest women in Europe. Also 46 years old. Daughter of Heinrich Thyssen and Baroness Margareta Bornemisza de Kászon. Granddaughter of the German steel baron August Thyssen. Mad about horses, and happiest when she is out hunting.

MARITTA   My grandmother. 34 years old. A heavy smoker. Survived the battle of Budapest, in which 160,000 died at the end of the Second World War, in the catacombs of the city. Mother of a fourteen-year-old son (my father). After the war her family lost all its possessions, its status, and all its landed property. Before escaping to the West, she had been living with farming people in the Hungarian provinces.

FERI   My grandfather. In 1957 he is 42 years old. He was called up in 1942, went to Poland and later the Ukraine, and fought in the Hungarian army beside the

Germans in the battle of the Don, where 60,000 died, most of them freezing to death in the trenches. Just before the end of the war he was picked up by the Russian army when he was only 50 kilometres from home, imprisoned, and sent to Western Siberia. Finally he was held in the little town of Asbest, where he had to quarry rock containing asbestos and lost his hair. He was set free after ten years, and is a devout Catholic.

THE TIME   Mid-February 1957. As a result of the Suez Crisis, US President Dwight D. Eisenhower has announced that the USA will protect pro-Western states from communist infiltration by all possible means. The war of independence is raging in Algeria. In Budapest, the show trials of those involved in the people's uprising have begun. In Munich a few weeks later, Erich Kästner's play *School for Dictators* has its première, Elvis Presley is playing in Jailhouse Rock, and in Liverpool the Cavern Club, where the Beatles will soon make headlines, has opened. The Hungarian regent Miklós Horthy, who governed the country during the war and made a pact with the Germans until mid-1944, has been dead for less than a week.

THE PLACE   The Villa Mita, 6906 Castagnola, Lugano

These four people, all still relatively young, all with their different previous lives, sit down at the dining table together. Jóska brings in a steaming tureen of fish soup. Feri can hardly restrain his delight, Ivan adjusts the position of his chair. Margit has her plate filled first: dark brown broth with pale green rings of leeks in it, pieces of fish with reddish fibres. 'Good soup, this,' says Feri at last. 'Home-made always tastes best,' says Ivan, who can't bear silence.

IVAN   Have I told you yet that we're going to become Swiss citizens?*

* AN: In 1958, Ivan and Margit engaged the well-known lawyer Ferruccio Bolla, a member of the Swiss Liberal Party and the upper house of the Swiss parliament, to

49

FERI   No, I didn't know. Right away?

IVAN   We're in no great hurry, but I think we'll apply for citizenship next year.

FERI   Is it as easy as that?

IVAN   Easy as pie. We're not just anyone.*

AUNT MARGIT   Just imagine, you have to answer questions about history and geography to become Swiss. Who was William Tell? And why, for goodness' sake, do they speak three languages in this tiny country?

MARITTA   Four. You're forgetting . . .

AUNT MARGIT   Three or four, what does it matter? Anyway, it's absurd to expect me to read history books. As if I had time for such things.†

---

have them naturalized. The first obstacle was Ivan's Uruguayan citizenship, which he wanted to keep.

* AN: The Castagnola police visited the couple in their villa, and questioned them for a long time, going into their financial assets, among other things. The first sum mentioned was only 500,000 francs, but it rose steadily in the course of their application, and was set at one point as three million and later at thirty-one million Swiss francs.

† AN: Ivan answered all the questions about civics knowledgeably, but that did him no good. The authorities in Berne did not agree to his petition for citizenship. Not yet. Two years later the lawyer Ferruccio Bolla tried again. Once more he dwelt on the love that Ivan and Margit felt for Switzerland, Ivan mentioned his subscriptions to the *Neue Zürcher Zeitung* and the *Corriere del Ticino*, as well as his membership of the Lugano Golf Club, the Corviglia Ski Club in St. Moritz, and the Bernina Section of the Swiss Alpine Club, but it got him no further. A note in the file about the second rejection runs: 'We have the impression that Batthyány wants citizenship for his own advantage. As we see it, the recurrent petitioner represents the perfect type of a cosmopolitan foreigner who lives now in one country, now in another, depending on his interests and his fantasies, and is at home everywhere and nowhere. People of that kind, in general prosperous, are inclined to think that everything, even a nationality, can be bought with money or the influence that money provides.'

Two years later, it finally worked. The officials did still assume that there was a

MARITTA   There are worse ways to spend your time.

AUNT MARGIT   You think so? This country should consider itself lucky to have us here, considering the taxes we pay. We also bring international flair to Ticino. We are making Lugano a meeting place for important people, actors, artists.* Maybe that hotelier in St. Moritz could help, what was his name? Help me, Ivan. Oh, there's no bearing this.

IVAN   Badrutt?

AUNT MARGIT   No, he died long ago. Or did he? Oh, children, children, I have to do everything for myself.

FERI   Who's dead?

Jóska, the butler whom Margit and Ivan have brought from Rechnitz with them, a quiet, reserved man, will also have known a good deal about the crime against those 180 Jews, but was never questioned. He clears away the soup plates and brings in the main course: braised beef with fried potatoes. Ivan pours red wine. The conversation lapses, which does not trouble the two ladies, but Ivan is searching desperately for a subject.

'largely cosmopolitan element' in Ivan's petition, but they gave it the green light. In June 1970, Ivan and Margit Batthyány-Thyssen became Swiss citizens.

There are two remarkable features of this twelve-year attempt to get citizenship. The Swiss authorities say not a word about the Rechnitz massacre in their records, either in direct questioning or in a note in the files, although the Federal Swiss police knew about Rechnitz. It is also odd that during their application Margit always kept in Ivan's shadow, which was not her style in real life. The wife over-shadowed by her husband. Did she have something to hide?

* AN: Margit's brother, Hans Heinrich Thyssen, extended his father's art collection, and in 1949 opened it to the public in the Villa Favorita in Lugano, in Margit's neighbourhood. In 1993 he sold the collection, which contained works by Rodin, Titian, and many other artists, to Spain. Today it can be seen in the Museo Thyssen-Bornemisza in Madrid.

IVAN   There's something we wanted to discuss. We thought that now you've settled in so well here, Feri, you could, well, only if your health permits it . . . I mean . . .

AUNT MARGIT   What Ivan's trying to say is that I need a private secretary. Someone to look after my business affairs. The buildings, the papers, the securities – it's all so complicated. It wasn't like that before the war.

FERI   You want me to work for you? (*Looks at his wife.*)

IVAN   You could find yourselves a nice apartment in Lugano. You've been so cold, ever since you came back from Siberia, and Ticino is considered the sunroom of Europe.

MARITTA   It's kind of you to think of us. (*Looks at her cigarettes.*)

FERI   So I'd be . . .

IVAN   You'd be our accountant.

AUNT MARGIT   My accountant.

IVAN   That's what I mean.

MARITTA   But we don't want to be a burden on you. And what will become of . . .

AUNT MARGIT   Your son? We'll send him to the Rosenberg boarding school in St Gallen; we've made arrangements. You couldn't do better. They even have tennis courts. The boy does play tennis, doesn't he?

MARITTA   Football.

AUNT MARGIT   Everyone sends their children to St Gallen these days. The school isn't exactly cheap, but we'll see to that. Children need a good education, especially now the economy is doing well again. I'm sure, my dear, that you agree with me – *d'accord?* (*Looks at Maritta.*)

MARITTA   I'm just rather surprised that the two of you have already – but yes, of course.

AUNT MARGIT   The child must go to school.* He can't go on lounging around doing nothing and hiding from the challenges of life. He always seems so despondent. Where's the wine? (*Picks up the handbell from the table and rings it.*) Jóska!

MARITTA   He doesn't hide from challenges. (*Aunt Margit is still ringing the bell energetically.*)

AUNT MARGIT   What did you say?

JÓSKA?   Yes, madam?

AUNT MARGIT   The wine, Jóska, the wine.

MARITTA   Maybe it's difficult for you to understand, because . . .

JÓSKA   Of course, madam.

MARITTA . . .   because he's gone through a great deal for a boy of fourteen. He hardly knows his father (*looks at Feri*). It hasn't been easy for us. It isn't like Switzerland in Hungary.

AUNT MARGIT   We have all suffered, my child, not just you two. We ourselves have lost a great deal.

* AN: My father went to school in St Gallen until he took his school-leaving certificate, and later studied chemistry in Zürich.

IVAN   Never mind the old days now. Women shouldn't talk about politics, it doesn't suit you. Let's celebrate instead. A wonderful future lies ahead of us. Do you know what the best thing about Switzerland is? Its situation. Portobello, Vienna, Paris – you can get to them all in just a few hours.

And so the evening goes on. After the wine there is cognac, and chocolate with it. A family friend, Eduard von der Heydt,* brought it back from Ascona recently.

As I imagine the scene above, Ivan and Feri go on to discuss their little spin over the green border to Italy next day. Ivan says that the forests there are teeming with wild boar. Feri doesn't really see why he should go trudging around the countryside in this cold weather, when he would rather spend the day beside the fire on the hearth, but out of politeness he agrees. They excuse themselves from the table, and go to study maps of northern Italy.

The two women are left behind. They smoke, sip from their glasses, and talk idly about this and that. Although suppose they don't? Suppose they break their silence and open up to each other? But why would they do that?

It is not in Margit's interests to talk about Rechnitz, and why would my grandmother have confided in her, of all people? Perhaps because they have both had too much to drink? No.

Perhaps because they are tired of acting as if everything were perfectly all right, as their menfolk do? That is more likely.

Suppose their defences came down for a few minutes? Suppose

---

* AN: Eduard von der Heydt, a very rich banker's son, was a member of the National Socialist Party for six years. He became a Swiss citizen in 1937, and left the Party two years later. Von der Heydt bought Monte Verità in Ascona, was a patron of artists and writers, and became a member of the Swiss League of Loyal Confederates, a party very close to National Socialism. During the war he did business deals for the Nazis in Lugano, which did not trouble anyone, for the Ticino authorities were not rigorous in their investigations. Later, he collected works of art, particularly from China and Africa, and bequeathed them to the city of Zürich. They can be seen in the Rietberg Museum today.

all the words that my grandmother kept bottled up came bursting out of her: all her grief; her anger with herself for failing to help the Mandls; the leaden years under communism; her difficulties with her husband and this new world order; her hatred of conspicuous consumption, coasters with horse patterns on them, cheerful people like Ivan who have the nerve to take life easily?

Suppose, on that day in mid-February 1957, let's say at 22.15 in the evening, this remark had been made?

MARITTA   I can't bear it any more. I can't deal with the guilt of it.

AUNT MARGIT   What guilt? I don't know what you're talking about. (*Falls silent.*)

MARITTA   I do. (*She falls silent too.*)

Goaded by Aunt Margit's coldness that stifles all humanity in her, my grandmother tells her about that afternoon in the inner courtyard of the castle, talking herself into a fury. She wants to provoke Margit. She wants a reaction. She tells her about the Mandls, the scream, how they asked her father to help them. She will have spoken the phrase 'fellow travellers' once, twice – it could have been like that. Why not?

MARITTA   We are all fellow travellers. That's what we are, fellow travellers. But it's too easy to claim that we had to obey. What was our own part in those terrible deeds?

The clock on the wall strikes twice. It is ten-thirty.

AUNT MARGIT   Do you know what I can't stand about you aristocrats? It's the way you always take everything personally. Do you think yourselves better than the rest of us? First you look down on everyone, and then, when times are harder, you give way like newborn lambs. Jóska! (*Silence.*)

JÓSKA   Yes, madam?

AUNT MARGIT   A bottle of sparkling wine.

JÓSKA   Of course.

AUNT MARGIT   You have no idea what we went through in Rechnitz back
    then, just before the end of the war. And while they were all scared silly, my hus-
    band first and foremost, someone had to keep calm and get the work done. Do
    you know why I like horses better than human beings? Because they like being
    trained. No backbone, my dear, that's what the world is suffering from.

Jóska opens a bottle and fills two slender glasses. Ivan and Feri come
back, still discussing the possibility of going to Italy by the alternative
Arogno route. 'In which car?' Ivan is heard to murmur. And what if it
snows, whispers my grandfather in Hungarian: '*Mi van, ha esik a hó?*'

'Well, what have you been chatting about, my loves?' asks Ivan,
and he looks at the table, seeing red wine stains on the tablecloth,
ash beside the ashtray, and two glasses of sparkling wine. 'Not politics again, surely?'

'Life,' replies Aunt Margit. 'And Feri's position as my private
secretary. Maritta thought it might be better if they went to Germany after all rather than staying with us, isn't that so, Maritta?'

My grandmother nods and smokes, and stares straight ahead.

'I'll see if I can do something,' says Aunt Margit. 'It should be
possible to find a post in one of the Thyssen works somewhere in the
Ruhr.'*

---

* AN: And it was. My grandparents moved to Dinslagen, a small town near Düssel-
dorf, where my grandfather had the position of company secretary with power of
attorney to one of the Thyssen plants.

7

'How's the dog?' I asked my father over the phone.

'Crazy,' he replied. 'Out of control. In the car he jumps on the front seats and sits on my knee. I'll have to take him to the Animals' Home.'

'Poor thing. But a bit of exercise would do you good.'

'Never mind me, how about you? How are your investigations into Aunt Margit going?'

'Word has obviously gone around about them. I get phone calls from family members. Where did they get my number? From you?'

'Are you joking?'

'"Why dig up the past?" they ask. They say it would do more harm than good if I made more about Margit known. They're threatening me.'

'And what do you tell them?'

'I say that we can come to terms with the past only if we keep saying what happened. That's not my own idea, of course, it comes from Hannah Arendt.'

'Oh, her.'

'Do you agree with them that all this searching won't get me anywhere?'

'No, but I doubt whether our relations know anything.'

'That's the point. No one knows anything because no one has ever asked. Isn't that odd? You all knew about that massacre, and you knew that Aunt Margit was there, but you were too polite to ask questions. You didn't want to fall out of favour with her.'

'Wait a minute.'

I heard the click of a cigarette lighter and a rustling; he must have dropped the receiver. Then I heard his voice again. 'Are you still there?'

'Of course I'm still here. It's the money, right?'

'What?'

'The money kept you all quiet. Aunt Margit paid, so she had power. She decided what would be mentioned – and what wouldn't. Aunt Margit had you all in the hollow of her hand.'

*

I last went to the Burgenland at the end of autumn. It was misty, the houses, the fields, the sky were all grey, and the bunches of grapes had been harvested long ago. All Saints' Day was coming, and the family met to remember their dead forebears in the family vault below the monastery church of Güssing. A dark room with dozens of coffins containing those forebears, some dusty with time, others more recent. 'Do you want to lie here some day?' I was asked in the light of a candle by someone who introduced himself as my cousin.

After we had climbed the steps again, we all sat down at a long wooden table: aunts, uncles, cousins, people I hardly knew.

Most of them could remember Margit and Ivan very well: their travels, their houses, Margit's horses and Ivan's vanity. And the longer I sat at the table with them the more comfortable I felt. The way they talked, their jokes, the old furniture, the porcelain, the little silver sugar bowl – it was all familiar.

'What the newspapers say is nonsense,' the older ones claimed. Elfriede Jelinek's play *Rechnitz: The Exterminating Angel*, about Rechnitz and Margit, gives a misleading impression, they say. Margit had nothing to do with the massacre, I was told. 'She was unpopular and dependent on men,' they said; she was obsessed with sex – but a murderess? 'Certainly not.' I nodded, we all nodded. And when one of the party, an elderly man who had greeted me in a friendly way although we didn't know each other, talked about Jews and Jewish propaganda, everyone stopped listening and acted as if they didn't know what he was talking about. I held my tongue myself, and I did not contradict him when he said, 'Maybe the massacre never took place at all?'

We drank black tea and ate ham rolls.

All the people at the table were now talking at once: about the mass grave, about the search. The younger ones asked questions, the older ones avoided the subject.

'What's the point of it all?'

'Why bother?'

'What's it to do with us?'

A general shaking of heads.

Silence.

'Would anyone like more tea?'

No one spoke up.

'There's been enough written already about crimes against the Jews,' the old man defended himself. 'The crimes of the communists were just as bad.' And once again the subject was ignored; no one wanted to go into it. 'Jelinek is Jewish herself, that's why she writes such garbage.' Someone cracked a joke to lighten the atmosphere, and everyone laughed, including me, the way you do laugh and nod in families. Two hours later we went our separate ways.

Once again there were friendly embraces; these people, this furniture, those cups, all so familiar to me. 'Do think about the family's good name,' an uncle who had sat there in silence all through the evening said to me. 'You don't want to drag it through the mud.' Almost affectionately, he took me by the chin and put his hand to my cheek just as my father always does. Later, in the car, I felt terrible.

Were many of them indifferent to the crime because it was about the murder of Jews?

I phoned my father. 'Is that what you think, too?'

'No, I don't.'

'Why those remarks about the Jews and Elfriede Jelinek?'

'Your uncle compared the crimes of the Nazis to the crimes of the communists. That's legitimate.'

'But why the jokes about Jews?'

'Are you going to write about that family visit?' asked my father. 'That will make for bad blood.'

'I don't know yet.'

A few weeks later I was standing by Aunt Margit's grave in Lugano, trying to remember her face and failing. The wind blew the last leaves off the trees, and all I could picture was her tongue.

It is a plain grave in Castagnola cemetery, at the foot of Monte Brè – a simple granite slab, although Margit was one of the richest women in Europe, and modesty was not a virtue of hers. '21 June 1911 – 15 September 1989. Margit Batthyány-Thyssen.' Someone had brought her yellow chrysanthemums; the earth in the pot was fresh.

After the conversations I had had with my family, with eyewitnesses and with my father, all the files, all the travelling, I was sure now that Aunt Margit had not shot anyone on that moonlit night of 24 March 1945, a month before Hitler's suicide. She did not murder any Jews, as the newspapers claimed she did. There is no evidence. There are no witnesses.

Aunt Margit did not stand in the cold at midnight beside that pit where the naked men and women were kneeling in a row. She was laughing and dancing as their emaciated bodies fell into the ground. She laughed and danced with the murderers when they returned to the castle at three in the morning.

And while, somewhere in Rechnitz, the 180 bodies were mouldering in a pit, Aunt Margit went on a cruise ship every year across the summery blue Aegean Sea, drank kir royal in Monte Carlo, and hunted deer in the autumnal forests of the Burgenland.

Aunt Margit enjoyed the rest of her long life, although she knew everything about the massacre. Rotten seed.

8

In the middle of November I was going to fly to Moscow with my father, to learn more about the gulag and Stalin's reign of terror, and find the camp where my grandfather had spent ten years of his life. 'Won't it be too cold?' my father asked on the phone, although we'd discussed it so often before. 'I don't have any warm shoes,' I heard him sighing.

'Nor do I,' I replied.

In my imagination, I saw us walking over the fields, laughing, I threw a snowball at him, and we told one another stories that we didn't already know from each other, the way good friends do.

But when I thought about it more closely, I saw us sitting at a table in the breakfast room of a dismal hotel somewhere in the country, unable to converse as we took the tops off our soft-boiled eggs in silence.

'I'm still close to my father physically,' I told Strassberg a few days after our conversation. 'We hug and kiss whenever we meet. Even as a child I liked to feel his warm hands on my cheeks, his fingers, with their smell of nicotine, intertwined with mine. It's easier for us to touch than to talk. Why would that be so?' I asked. 'It wouldn't trouble me to look after him in his old age, give him soup, wash and dress him,' I went on, seeing pictures in my mind's eyes of myself lifting him out of the shower like a small child. 'But what I can't stand is sitting in a plane or spending six hours in the car with him. And I think he feels the same about me. Why?'

'Go on that trip and find out,' said Strassberg. He could

sometimes be very down to earth, which annoyed me, because I felt he was showing me up.

'It's like a physical pain, if you see what I mean. Simply sitting there, feeling that I could be close to him, but I just don't know how.'

'What do you expect of those few days in Russia?'

'I hope the situation will resolve itself. I'd like the burden of it to disappear. I want to walk down the streets with him without having to wonder, all the time, what I ought to do or say now. When I think of my father and myself, I see in my mind's eye those round magnets that you stick to the fridge. Do you know the feeling when you're trying to press one on top of the other?'

'Of course.'

'One of them always gives way and moves aside. The space between them, just a few millimetres, is only air, or so you think, it all looks so simple, but you can't get the two to stick together. It's like that with me and my father. I wish the space between us would go away.'

'Time's up, I'm afraid,' he said, and yet again I felt embarrassed to have revealed myself, and then be brought abruptly down from the clouds into real life. I heard him getting out of his armchair behind me; it always sounded as if he were swinging his torso forward first and using the momentum to get on his feet. We shook hands quickly. I would have preferred a hug.

Diaries III

Agnes

They crammed us into freight trucks like cattle. We were all unwashed, we had worn the same clothes since we were in Budapest. The doors were bolted; there were no windows. We set off: children, old people, women, all crowded close together. Many of us were weeping, others screaming, two people died. When the train stopped, days later, we were relieved. We had finally reached Auschwitz.

When we got out, we were surrounded by nurses and doctors. One of them must have been Dr Mengele. Someone shouted, 'Anyone who doesn't feel well come this way, please, the others go over there.' The doctors came and looked us up and down. Small children were torn away from their mothers.

My husband – I didn't know him yet at the time – arrived at the same ramp, as he told me later. He had met his first wife in the Łodz ghetto, and they had a son eight months old. When the guards tried taking the baby away from his wife on the ramp, she fought back, so they gassed both mother and child.

Those of us who still had our strength were ordered to walk on. Soon we were faced by new buildings, new huts, new guards, barbed wire everywhere: Birkenau. They led us into a room where we had to undress and be tattooed. From that moment on I had no name any more, I was only a number. But thanks to the German nanny who lived with us when I was still at home with my parents, I understood what I had to do. All the others, who didn't know German, had more difficulty. Those who couldn't say what their number was were punished, or simply did not appear again one morning. Was it that German nanny, of all people, who saved my life?

After the tattooing we went to shower, and after that German soldiers shaved our heads. I had never before in my life been treated with such contempt. Once back in the fresh air, showered, tattooed, our heads shaven, we were different people. There were mothers who didn't recognize their own daughters.

Maritta

It was Rogation Sunday, and instead of going to church we and the priest assembled in the fields once a year. He went ahead, we followed him, and he blessed the earth so that it would give us a good harvest. Most of the women from the village were there, the old people, we children, and also my father, but not my mother. Where was she all that time? We were standing on a rise in the ground, looking out at the landscape. I saw the marshes, the forests that I knew well from hunting, and suddenly one of the village women pointed to a train that had more trucks than usual behind the engine. It was clearly visible. I can remember how the sun made the roof of the train sparkle. Our priest also looked, and when someone said, 'The Jews are in there,' we couldn't tear our eyes away. Everyone looked at the trucks glittering in the sunlight. The priest moved on, and we followed him until Mass was over.

At the time hardly anyone knew that I was pregnant with a second child. A few months before, Feri had been given a week's leave, and we had met in Budapest. He didn't know how to get on with his first child – how could he, when he was away all the time? And soon he was to have a second one.

There was very little news in the countryside. We had just a single crackly radio, and everything seemed so far away, so unreal, although we ourselves had German soldiers billeted on the home farm, military trucks drove through the village, and a swastika flag flew from the roof of the village hall. My father had no objection to the Germans, indeed he liked them, although that didn't make him a Nazi. He certainly wasn't an anti-Semite, he just liked the German sense of order and punctuality.

He had been to agricultural fairs in Berlin several times before the war, and came back in a state of great excitement, as if he had travelled into the future. He was not a political man. He didn't think about the deportations, he knew nothing of the terrible things going on. His real interests were hunting, nature, the forest. Thinking of him today, I realize that he liked animals better than human beings.

It was not our parents who brought us up, listened to us and received our confidences, but the domestic staff, people like our lady's maid Goga, who looked after us and answered our questions. I would have found it hard to survive my childhood and youth without Goga. She was the heart of the house. She picked us the first snowdrops and violets, brought us fresh tea when we caught a cold, or the first strawberries from the market garden. She is woven into every pattern, every path, every image of my younger days. Goga was still full of energy, she made tea for everyone, was always ready to lend a hand, organized things and was in charge, but by now she was more bent that I remembered her in my childhood. She was touchy, disgruntled, and I once saw her smoking in the garden. Goga, who never drank, didn't even eat chocolate because she thought it was a sin, was now drawing quickly on a filterless cigarette.

But the household rules were still what they had always been. Every morning we breakfasted at the long table with my father, even now. We didn't talk much. Goga went to church every Friday afternoon, and then the Rosary Society met, with the priest in charge. In those days, as I remember it, the weather was either blazing hot or cold with snow falling. After prayers the members of the Rosary Society went up to the altar one by one, took pieces of paper, and wrote numbers corresponding to Biblical verses on them. Goga always used to put those rolled-up notes on our pillows. As far back as I can remember, Friday evening was linked to them; I would unroll mine before going to bed, and then open the Bible. I was a devout child, indeed I was.

Agnes

They woke us at five in the morning, and gave everyone a job to do. Once we had to carry a large pile of stones away. We heaved the stones into wheelbarrows, pushed them to the other side of the camp, and unloaded them there. Next day we were told to bring them all back again.

It was still cold all the time outside. I remember someone I didn't know coming to me and giving me the present of a pair of second-hand socks. I was astonished, and so grateful that I couldn't make up my mind whether to wear them on my hands or my feet, so I shared the socks between them alternately.

There was hardly anything to eat. After we got up, they gave us a cup of a brew that the Germans called coffee. It was brown, but that was all it had to do with real coffee. A tiny piece of bread was doled out with it. At mid-day there was what we called 'meadow soup', because it was greenish, and had no flavour, but you can get used to anything. Days passed in the same routine. I once asked a girl who had been there for four years whether anyone had ever left the camp alive, to which she replied, 'No one ever gets out of this camp.' So far, however, I had been spared illness, I had neither diarrhoea nor lice, and I swore to myself that I was not going to die here.

Maritta

The war reached our village in November 1944. The Russians were coming closer and closer, the Hungarians and Germans were trying to hold back the Red Army. I returned to Budapest because I was told I would be safer there. The Russians hated aristocrats, so my parents left the castle, and went to stay at a monastery in Zirc, a small town in the west of the country. My second son, Béla, had been born by now.

The city was full of soldiers and trucks, there were wounded men everywhere, and people on the road with all their worldly goods. It was cold, there wasn't much to eat, and everyone, including me, wanted to go up to the Castle district. Life went on there, in contrast to the other districts of the city. Even the Ruszwurm cake-shop was still open. There was a small market where people bartered goods with each other, we all talked to everyone else, and the men drank far too much schnapps, as always in our country. Schnapps is the great evil of Hungary, although not the only one.

In the evening we would sit on a bench, looking down at the city below, and seeing several buildings burning. We knew we would be next. And when the Soviets took all of Pest, everything was suddenly very quiet up near the Castle. As if we were all holding our breath.

Agnes

The only thing I brought to the camp from my former life was a photo of my family. On the first day, when we all had to undress and they tattooed us, I asked the guards to let me keep the photo, but they took it away from me. A few weeks later it was lying on my bed. It's strange, but even in the concentration camp there were miracles and moments of happiness. I don't know who gave it back to me, or why. Maybe someone just found it? Maybe someone felt sorry for me? I was happy, but I didn't know where to keep it, and above all I was afraid of tearing it. I found an empty margarine box somewhere between the huts, and I sewed the photo into it, using a bit of wire and the seam of a piece of clothing. It would last better there. But every time I looked at it, I felt such a pang of grief that I finally gave it to another girl, asking her to keep it for me.

I could neither talk about my family nor bear it when others talked about theirs. One morning we all had to stand in a row, and I realized that they were separating the taller, stronger and healthier women from the weaker ones. I asked the girl who had my photo to give it back to me. She looked so thin and ill. I never saw her again, and after that I always kept the photo with me.

Maritta

We were planning to spend three days in the catacombs of the Castle district. We prepared for our stay: my cousin carried champagne into the cellar by the crate, saying that there'd be no joking with the Russians, and we all laughed. Those three days turned into five weeks.

There were ten of us in our cellar hideout, a little room with a candle burning in one corner. The children screamed, and were smelly, but we didn't have enough water to change and wash their nappies. We expected the Russians to turn up any day now. We discussed what it would be like when they knocked, when they came in. What will become of us, we wondered, what more can happen? We heard bombs exploding in the distance, and salvoes of machine-gun fire.

Sometimes someone brought us news.

Churchill was said to have met Stalin by the Black Sea, and many of us thought that was good news. Others didn't. I didn't mind either way. I was sitting on a mattress, my elder son was asleep, his little brother was crying. My breast milk had dried up days ago. I tried sugared water, but Béla wouldn't drink it; he retched and coughed.

Agnes

They took us to a shower room. Sometimes gas came out of the shower heads, sometimes water. That time it was water.

Maritta

Someone told me I ought to rub my breasts with curd cheese because they were inflamed, but where was I going to find curd cheese? Béla was getting more and more tired. He would sleep in my arms for hours, until he hardly opened his eyes.

Agnes

When we came out of the shower room, Mengele and a couple of other doctors were facing us. They examined us all over, looked into all our orifices. We were scarecrow figures, human beings without any flesh on our bones. They gave us new clothes, left by some of the dead.

Maritta

The Russian who found us was short and round-shouldered, with a Mongol face and a ragged fur cap on his head. He broke open the cellar door and ran down the steps, his steps thudding, and we heard the first Russian words spoken. 'It's starting now,' said my cousin, and just this once he was to be proved right. Something did start then: 45

devastating years of communism. But not much happened at that moment itself. I was afraid. We were all afraid. Béla was asleep; his face very hot; we had no candles left, and an oil lamp, burning faintly, left an acrid smell in the air. The Russian had a remarkably refined voice. He said he was looking for *nemez* – Germans; he sounded like a boy. In fact it was German women he was after. He let me go.

Agnes

They locked us up in a hut for three weeks. We still got some food, but we had nothing to do and no idea what would happen now. At the end of those three weeks, in the evening, they told us to go with them. They gave us each a piece of the bread that we knew so well, and some canned meat. We got into a train. The trucks were empty except for a bucket to use as a toilet, and a little straw on the floor. And for the first time I fell sick, with colitis. I spent the whole journey sitting on that bucket, for two days. Until the train stopped and we were told to get out. There were 155 of us. And we were the first 155 inmates ever to leave Auschwitz alive.

Maritta

When the Russian had gone, we crawled out of our hiding-place. You could see people everywhere clambering out of the ruins, like rats in the night. I had no idea where to go, until a family member advised me to take the children to my mother-in-law. The part of the city where her apartment was had been destroyed, windows broken, the roof bombed, with an icy wind blowing through the cracks. There were only two rooms, and a single bed on which my mother-in-law was lying. She was crippled by recent events, and croaked as if she were snoring. That was all the sound anyone heard from her. To make tea you had to bear the croaking, because the coal-burning stove that also acted as an oven stood beside her bed. People were saying that the war was over, but we didn't know what would happen now.

It was a long time since I had heard anything from my parents. Let alone my husband.

Agnes

The train door opened. SS guards were standing on the platform; it was late in the evening and they ordered us to march along a small, unlit path. I was feeling very weak, I had diarrhoea and could hardly walk. But the other women in the group supported me and helped me back to my feet when I stumbled. German officers in the background were shouting, 'Get moving! Get moving!' I'll never forget those words. I don't know how I made it, but after a while, walking through the night, we did indeed come to a factory. A spinning mill. We were told not to let anyone know where we came from and what we had been through in Auschwitz. They led us into a room full of unmade beds where we could lie down and sleep. They were the beds of the women working on the night shift in the spinning mill, and when we went to work in the morning, they lay down there. We were well off by comparison with Auschwitz.

The supervisors of the shifts could choose the women they wanted working for them, so again we were examined and sorted and quarantined. It was now that some of the women discovered they were pregnant, because they stopped menstruating. They tried to hide it; pregnant women disappeared, and no one knew where they went.

Our supervisor asked us who knew German, and I was sent to the drying room, where I had to help hang up sixty to eighty kilos of heavy bales of fabric. That was my work now, day after day.

One morning I woke with terrible toothache. My supervisor

sent me off, with a soldier, to a dentist in the village. A notice on his door said, 'No Jews treated.' But we went in all the same. The dentist told me to open my mouth, picked up a pair of pincers, and pulled as hard as he could. All of this standing up. Minutes later we were outside again, but the pain got no better. I didn't have a mirror, but I soon realized that he had drawn the wrong tooth. Luckily there was a Jewish dentist whom the factory manager sent to see us once a month. I told him I thought I would die of the pain in my tooth. 'The war is nearly over,' he replied. 'Hang on.'

And then, suddenly, the factory was closed. We no longer had to dry textiles, we were told, we must help to build bunkers for the German population so that they would all be safe when the Allies dropped their bombs. Our work was very strenuous: we had to dig a trench with very few tools. There was a coalmine opposite where French prisoners of war were working; they handed us little notes saying that the war would soon be over. Several weeks passed like this, always with the same daily rhythm. Until the morning came when no one woke us. For the first time in months, there was only silence.

Maritta

For a while I was glad to have found a place to stay with my mother-in-law. In spite of the difficulty of those days, there were some cheerful moments, for instance when a cousin and I set off, with her baby's pram and mine, to steal coal. The whole city was a pile of rubble, the bridges lay sunk in the Danube. More cousins and other family members arrived every day, the apartment was more and more crowded, there were children everywhere playing hide and seek around the bed – what else were they to do?

Agnes

They usually knocked to rouse us at five in the morning, but nothing happened that day. We lay in those beds until three in the afternoon, when someone told us to go to one of the huts. The factory manager and an SS man were standing on a table with keys in their hands. 'We've had news,' they called. 'Germany has surrendered. The war is over.' They threw the keys away to show that it was finally all over. And what were we to do now?

Maritta

Most of the children in the apartment were undernourished, sick and weak, but they survived. Except for mine. Béla died on the day when the war ended.

9

A cold, icy wind blew towards us at Moscow Airport, as we fol-lowed our taxi driver across a large car park to his vehicle. 'For me, visiting Russia is like what a visit to Auschwitz must be for Jews,' my father told me, on the way to the hotel where a travel agency in Budapest had talked him into booking us: a grey tower building with a shopping arcade in front of it. The shops were either closed or hadn't even opened yet. We got out of the taxi, I pulled my father's wheeled suitcase through black puddles of rain outside the entrance, and joined the cluster of people at the reception desk, all of them brandishing their passports. There was a small bar in the lobby, and I had taken my father there so that he could rest from the flight, from his first impressions – yes, from what, really? I wanted to spare us a wait with Uzbek businessmen and truck drivers from Astana to col-lect the key to our room. I looked at him drinking his beer, an elderly gentleman in a grey winter jacket buttoned up to the neck, and his new shoes with their fake fur lining on view. He did not look at the TV set, or the other hotel guests hurrying past him. Nor was he interested in the brochures lying on the counter, all those shashlik restaurants in the vicinity, gaming casinos, striptease clubs – all he wanted to do was sit there. I don't know anyone else who can sit motionless for so long, staring straight ahead of him. A thought came into my mind that often used to pass before my inner eye in my youth, as if on a red LED ticker display: make sure he's all right. Only I never knew how to go about it.

How are you? I typed into my phone. We were less than twenty metres apart. I waited until the text reached him, and he jumped slightly because his mobile was vibrating. Where was it, inside his clothing, outside him? In the pocket of his trousers. He took his glasses off to read the message. I saw him writing back, his forefinger on the little display. I knew what the answer would be; it was an old joke between us. Every family has its code, and ours was: not too bad.

Not too bad, that used to be our reply to all kinds of questions. Everything was 'not too bad'. School, a meal, our moods. Have you had a good day? Not too bad. How was the tennis match? Not too bad, and how about you at the office? Nothing was ever really good; misfortune always threatened, and even if the sun happened to be shining, dark clouds would soon be sure to gather in the sky. My father would never have hyped anything, or made out that it was better than it was. There was a touch of loss and defeat about everything in my childhood, as if it might all fall apart at any time.

When we finally entered our room on the fourteenth floor, it was dark outside. I stood at the window and saw individual lights all the way to the horizon, with many black spaces between them. A small wood, maybe, or a park, probably also the graveyards of defunct cars, waste land, half-finished apartment blocks with iron rods sticking up into the air. 'There's a form of ugliness that I find attractive,' I said to my father, sounding like a student of architecture in his third semester, but I wanted to bridge the damn silence. 'Just as there are cities renowned for their beauty that put me off because they're too cute, if you see what I mean.' That sounded even worse; had I really said 'cute'? And because he didn't answer, I looked at him. He was lying on the bed, but not asleep. He hadn't even taken his jacket off, but his glasses were lying on the bedside table. Without them, he looked a different person.

*

My grandfather spent ten years in Russian captivity. From 1945 to 1955. The file on him at that time runs to almost a hundred pages. It had been lying in the military archives for sixty years by the time I found it, and had it photocopied and translated. There are two photographs in it, showing my grandfather as I have never seen him. One was taken soon after his arrest; it shows him at the age of thirty, wearing the kind of clothes favoured today by young hippies at organic markets in Brooklyn, Berlin and Zürich: a loose-knit pull-over with a lumberjack's shirt under it; a dark jacket; brown, calf-length lace-up boots. He looks healthy, has a light stubble, a high forehead, and not a trace of despair in his eyes, which are so like mine.

The second photograph dates from 1955, ten years later, and was taken in Camp 84, in a town called Asbest in the Ural mountains of Western Siberia. One Major Simanovsky had caught my grand-father breaking the camp rules. As reported on 1.4.1955: 'The convict Batthyány put his hand through the wire fence and tried to give Pris-oner T., in solitary confinement at the time, black bread with butter and sausage, 100 grams of sugar, and four cigarettes.'

Simanovsky wrote that he proposed seven days imprisonment for this offence. But my grandfather complained of fever and pain in the region of the kidneys. Simanovsky, a very conscientious guard, went to the trouble of checking his temperature. 'I make it only 37.3 degrees. He seems to be faking ill health,' I read aloud to my father in our hotel room, but he did not react. Was he asleep after all? Was he cursing himself, and wishing he were at home? I went on: 'His state of health will stand up to a week's imprisonment.' Simanovsky locked my grandfather up on 2 April, and let him out again on 9 April.

I wonder what became of Simanovsky? A faithful Soviet citi-zen, with Marx and Lenin on his bookshelves? Later on a civil servant, a member of the Communist Party, and by the time Gor-bachev came along, was he a senior citizen in a knitted cardigan with leather elbow patches, and a little dacha out in the country? Did he think of all the prisoners he had guarded while he whipped his back with a birch twig in the sauna at weekends?

Or maybe it was the other way around, and the years at the camp turned him against the regime. Marx and Lenin were banished to the cellar; instead he read Solzhenitsyn and the first political writings of Václav Havel, whom he secretly admired. Later he handed out leaflets and, when Gorbachev talked about *perestroika*, went out into the streets to rejoice. Did he remember all those prisoners while he listened to the slow movement of Tchaikovsky's Symphony No. 6, the Pathétique?

How many of those people are still around? I mean people like Simanovsky. They were young during the war, and in the eighties, when I was growing up, they were senior citizens with flat caps, age spots on their faces, and glasses with the sort of lenses that progressively darken in sunlight. All over Europe they fed pigeons, sat in the shade of large plane trees in parks, and patted the heads of strangers' babies in their prams. Forty years before, they had been guards, soldiers, secret policemen, informers, they had conducted interrogations, had tortured and murdered people, handed out severe sentences, and wrote up the records, just as Simanovsky wrote up my grandfather's. The photo taken of him in 1955, when he was imprisoned, no longer shows a hippy, but the kind of camp inmates we know from Spielberg films: head shaven, a few teeth missing, eyes dead. Without a word, I handed the photo to my father; we were both lying on our beds now. He held the picture so close to his eyes that the tip of his nose touched it, and it fluttered when he breathed out.

'What a miserable shit,' he said as I googled the name Simanovsky. Over 10,000 hits, among then a supplier of drinks near Red Square.

'Shall we go and have a drink?' I asked.

'At this time of night?'

'We're in Moscow, although it doesn't look like it from up here. There must be people somewhere, restaurants, cafés.'

'Are you sure?'

'No. All the same, I'm going down to Skype the children; I'll get better reception there.'

'Tell them hello from me.'

'They'll ask how Grandpa is – what do I say?'

'Say I'm not too bad.'

*

There were still dozens of people in the lobby; it would be like that all night. Russia is a country with eleven time zones, so people are arriving all round the clock to visit family or do business. I switched on my computer and, a little later, saw my wife and children crowding in front of the screen and all talking at once, so that I could hardly make anything out.

'Is there pasta in Russia too, Papa?' they asked.

'Has Grandpa seen a polar bear?'

At home I had told them how cold it is in Siberia, and they asked, 'As cold as where the polar bears live?' After a few minutes my wife sent the children away. 'Let me have a word too,' I heard her saying, and saw wobbly pictures. A knee? Hair? Then her voice. 'Off you go to your room now!' More shouting, and a door latching.

'Here I am,' she said. 'How's Moscow?'

'We haven't seen much of it. It's raining, and I don't have any warm shoes.'

'You should buy some, then.'

'Yes, I know.'

'How are things between you and your father?'

I felt like saying, 'Not too bad,' because it was exactly right, but instead I told her how depressed he seemed to be. 'Tired all the time,' I said, 'and taking no interest in anything. Am I like that myself?'

'Like what?'

'So withdrawn.'

'Give him a few more days,' she advised me, and I nodded.

'How are the children?'

'Complaining of sore throats.'

'Oh, hell.'

'It's not that bad.'

'Okay,' I said.

'Okay,' she replied. In the background I saw our living room, the green armchairs, the bookcase that we had discussed for ages before buying it. On the floor were the two rubber dinosaurs that we always trod on when one of the children had a bad dream at night, or was thirsty, and we had to get up to calm them down. One of the dinosaurs had wings and sharp teeth, the other a long, yellow neck. They were hardly recognizable on the screen, but I knew it was them. They belonged to our world.

'Look after yourself,' said my wife.

'I'll call from Siberia,' I replied, thinking that sounded good. A click, and she was gone.

10

My grandfather Feri was a lieutenant in the Hungarian army, which was under the control of the Germans, and fought side by side with them against the advancing Red Army. Feri's last position was in the vineyards of the town of Székesfehérvár, not far from Lake Balaton. When the defensive front against the Russians in Hungary gave way in January 1945, the only fighting still going on was around the capital city, and the Wehrmacht troops seemed to have disappeared overnight, he sent the men still under his command home, and set off himself by roundabout ways for the village of Sárosd, 25 kilometres away, where my grandmother Maritta and Agnes had grown up as near neighbours. My family's castle had already been bombed and looted, and the roof destroyed by fire. The house where Agnes used to live was still standing, but her parents' shop was empty, the windows boarded up, and her parents themselves were dead. People were so frightened that they stayed in their houses, the fields were neglected, the church closed, the gypsies had disappeared from the outskirts of the village, gone who knew where, whether to be gassed in a concentration camp or forgotten somewhere, with no one giving them another thought.

Feri took refuge with a farmer he knew. Several letters and documents from that time survive, and with their help the course of events can easily be reconstructed. He was on the point of burying his uniform when news came that all who had been in the Hungarian army were to report to Soviet headquarters to collect new ID cards. And because he wanted to reach Budapest and search for his wife and his sons, he went, but he left his gun, his watch and his wedding ring with the farmer. There were several witnesses to that.

The priest: 'I advised him against reporting to the Russians, and gave him a scrap of paper with a note of the time when the next train left for Budapest. But Feri wouldn't listen to me. 'I haven't done anything wrong,' he said, 'so what do you think could happen to me?'

The farmer: 'We did wonder whether it might be a trap, and discussed the possibility, but it's hard to hold back a man looking for his wife and children. He left his wedding ring, his watch and his gun with me, and his wife collected them all later.'

Peti, the coachman: 'The roads to Budapest were all under Russian control. But I tipped him off about the way to get to the capital without documents, by secret ways. I would have gone with him, I'd have done anything for the family, but he didn't want that.'

Of those three people, the village priest was closest to him, and knew all about the deaths of Herr and Frau Mandl. My grandmother had told him, in the confessional, what happened, mentioning the shots, and the pebbles flying into the air when Herr Mandl fell to the ground. She had said that she ought to have done something. 'Isn't that our duty?' she had cried through the grating in the wooden wall, and she suddenly began trembling because it was so incredibly cold. Then he had heard first her head striking the side of the confessional, and then the sound as she fainted away and fell from her chair.

But Feri would listen neither to him nor to the other two men. He did not realize how serious the situation was, didn't know what else might happen. After all, the war was almost over, everyone said so. Or was it his faith in God that told him to go? He must have set off to report to Russian HQ without another thought, and there he met a young Soviet lieutenant who spoke French and German, who did not shout but spoke politely, and whose job it was to interrogate all who had been in the Hungarian army. And because this lieutenant needed a Hungarian interpreter, he told my grandfather to go with him.

The name of the Russian with whom my grandfather spent the next few weeks was Efim Etkind. He was 27 years old at the time, and was later to become a highly regarded professor of literature. He had to leave the Soviet Union in the mid-seventies for political reasons. Etkind, the former Red Army soldier, was accused of possessing a manuscript copy of Alexander Solzhenitsyn's *The Gulag Archipelago*, an offence that made him guilty of treason. In addition, he was close to the writer Joseph Brodsky, who was critical of the Soviet system, and that was enough to arouse the attention of the KGB.

Efim Etkind and my grandfather were to meet again at the end of the nineties, when they were old men. By then the Cold War had ended long ago, Yeltsin was in power, the Soviet Union had collapsed. Etkind had a German wife; my grandfather was showing signs of dementia. The two white-haired figures who sat on a sofa together had seen fifty years of international history pass by.

But back then they were still young, and conducting interrogations somewhere in the Hungarian provinces. The war would soon be over. Etkind asked the questions, my grandfather translated, until the day when Etkind's company was recalled, probably in mid-February 1945.

My grandfather was handed over, in great haste, to the nearest assembly camp. He was no longer an interpreter there, but an ordinary prisoner. An area the size of a football field was surrounded by barbed wire, and new prisoners arrived every day. Did he realize, at that point, what was in store for him? Did he regret going to report to the village hall of his own free will? He had been so devout, said everyone who knew him well, one of the few who really felt imbued by his love of God. Feri was not a loud-mouthed man, not a leader, not a rebel. At the camp, he probably stood in a corner praying most of the time; yes, it could well have been like that. He put his trust in

God. Did he also ask where the hell God was in those years when millions of people died in Europe?

While my grandfather was in the assembly camp, thinking of his wife and children, Budapest went up in flames. Russian troops surrounded what was left of the German and Hungarian armies there, the dead lay in the streets, 150,000 people died, including 30,000 civilians. On 13 February, Russian soldiers hoisted the Soviet flag on Budapest Castle, and the battle was over.

Weeks after the last shot was fired, dead horses still lay in the streets. My grandmother and her children climbed over them on their way to her mother-in-law's apartment, which was in one of the few parts of the city still standing. Béla, her second son, was a babe in arms, pale and very thin. Singing troops passed by on the streets, trucks clattered by with the red star on their sides. Thieves, the wounded and starving people came to the window of the apartment, wanting to come into the warm, hoping for a little soup as well, but my grandmother, her brother-in-law, and all the others in the apartment who still had any strength left drove them away with cast-iron pans and broken bottles.

The war will soon be at an end, they said to give themselves hope, the time when human beings behave like wild animals will soon be over.

Then a man rang the doorbell. A Russian, a soldier. 'I have news of your husband,' he told my grandmother in French. He had dark hair, he was slender, and he seemed ill at ease. It was Efim Etkind. 'I met Feri. He worked for us as an interpreter.' He assured her that Feri was well, and would soon be back. 'We almost became something like friends,' he said, and went away again.

*

All this happened in those strange days just before the end of the war, when people did not yet understand what had happened to them. That spring, Agnes was working out of doors outside the spinning mill. She wore her concentration camp clothing, full of holes now, around her bony hips, she had a pickaxe to dig holes in the ground. Her new orders were to work on the building of bunkers. The German population must be kept safe from the Allies' air raids. So she raised the pickaxe in the air and brought it down on the cold ground, while in Budapest my grandmother Maritta cradled her second child in her arms, a baby who hardly moved and had stopped taking any nourishment, and Aunt Margit and Uncle Ivan in Rechnitz, that little Burgenland village, had champagne and wine brought up from the cellar because it seemed time to celebrate.

The first corks hit the ceiling in Rechnitz quite early. Margit and Ivan danced, and drank from full bottles; they were still young. Agnes was lying in a hut asleep one moonlit night at the end of March, when my grandmother buried her second child and told no one about it, and while my grandfather was sitting in a truck on the way to the gulag. And when a phone call came to Rechnitz at about midnight, saying there were 180 Jews at the railway station who must be disposed of, Aunt Margit and Uncle Ivan sent their staff to do the job for them.

A few days later the war really was over, and Hitler had shot himself. That moment, zero hour, began quietly: Agnes woke up on her thin mattress in a hut somewhere in Poland, and was surprised by the silence. No one knocking at the door, no morning roll-call, no shouting guards, only that strange peace. In Budapest, my grandmother packed her suitcase, took the hand of her remaining child, and left the apartment to look for her parents. When she turned the corner, she suddenly saw a torrent of humanity, dirty, hungry men and women on the way back to their children, their neighbours, their families. They came from concentration camps, prisons, field hospitals. They crawled out of hiding places, cellars, the ruins of bombed-out buildings.

Photographs of Eastern Europe at this time show apocalyptic scenes, cities destroyed, villages burnt, columns of smoke on the horizon, the remains of barbed wire in ditches, the abandoned huts of former camps in uncultivated fields, dead horses forgotten on marshy land.

In cities like Budapest, the air was full of the emanations from corpses. The bodies were bloated and did not smell of anything, said the survivors, but those emanations left a curiously soapy film on your skin, a fine layer that was difficult to wash off. However hard you scrubbed, your face, arms and legs were immediately covered with it again.

The man who had rung the doorbell of the apartment where my grandmother was staying, the shy, courteous Russian Efim Etkind, had been wrong about one thing: it was to be ten years before my grandfather arrived back in Budapest.

*

Feri was taken first to the Russian garrison town of Voronezh and Camp 82, Section 6, 500 kilometres from Moscow. There are no accounts of his journey, but it could have been like the one described by the Hungarian writer István Örkény, in his book *People of the Camps*. Like my grandfather, he was in Russian captivity. As he describes it, more than thirty men were sitting on the floor of a truck, all crammed into it together, and several of them on a plank bed, when another man was thrown in. Both his legs had been amputated; he had once been a doctor and a good swimmer. There was still a little room for him on the plank bed. On the sixth day of the rail journey, its fixings suddenly came loose and one end of the bed dropped to the floor as the train shook. The amputee's wounds had not healed yet; it was difficult for even a scratch to heal in those times. The man slid off, screaming.

Sometimes another man in the truck would bring himself to push him back and prop the slope of the bed up with a piece of wood, but that did not do much good. They would have had to lift the plank bed and nail it back in place, but no one roused himself to do that. The cripple whimpered for another two days and then fell silent. The others were unmoved by his cries of pain and his death.

None of them showed any sympathy for their companions, each was close only to himself, they functioned out of sheer instinct. Memory was suspended, or simply ceased entirely. Not only did faces and images fade, so did the names of those once loved, and important dates in their lives. Many thought that was the result of typhoid fever, but no: it was sheer indifference.

In 1948, three years after his arrest, and thus in the year when the communists came to power in Hungary, a time when my grandmother Maritta had to accept that an epoch had come to an end, and the whole social order of the past was turned upside down, my grandfather Feri was condemned to death in Voronezh. The verdict said that he and other soldiers in the Hungarian army had beaten up innocent citizens in the village of Ilovka, and shot a man called Dyuretski. Several witnesses claimed to have recognized him.

Batthyány, Ferenc / Number 34897534
Place of birth: Kittsee, 1915
Height: medium
Figure: slender
Neck: long
Face: pointed
Ears: small, round, prominent
Profession: lawyer
Military rank: lieutenant, company commander in the
    Hungarian army, 206th artillery division
Other details: descended from a princely family, owners of
    landed estates

'I am innocent,' he said at his trial, and he refused to sign the verdict.

'Aren't you a count?' he was asked.

'Yes.'

'Then tell us how you exploited the proletarians.'

'I've never exploited anyone.'

'Are you a count or aren't you?'

'Can I help it if I am?'

'Hold your tongue.'

Two years later the verdict was revised, and the death sentence commuted to life imprisonment. Stalin showed mercy, and Feri was transferred to Camp 362 in Stalingrad. 'State of health: good; epidemic sicknesses suffered: none,' say the transfer papers, with the remark: 'Stringent regime required.'

A year later he was moved to the Sverdlovsk district, near Yekaterinburg in the Ural mountains, first to Revda, then to a town called Asbest, where he quarried stone from the permafrost with his bare hands. Its fibres were later used in the construction of buildings, and caused cancer.

Diaries IV

Agnes

What did we do on the day when the war ended? After the manager of the factory had thrown away the keys and told us we were all free, we ran out of the door. The same guards for whom we had been working all this time, and whose orders we had to obey, were now standing at the factory gates doling out soup.

Later on that extraordinary day, we went for a drive with some Russian soldiers in their tanks. They gave us bread and bacon, and showed us how to salute in Russian. And when it grew dark we went back to our huts. Where else were we to spend the night? But there were Russians lying in wait for us; it was terrible. They had run wild, no one could control them, and they weren't taking orders any more. But even then I was lucky, because one of the girls in our group spoke a little Russian. She said that our huts were a kind of hospital ward, and we were all suffering from severe inflammations. That was how we discovered that only one thing would stop the Russians: their fear of infectious illness.

Maritta

While I spent the war in a cellar in Budapest, just before the Red Army reached our village my parents had fled to the Cistercian monastery of Zirc, a small town in the west of Hungary. They spent the worst of the war in relative safety there. A little later, in April 1945, I went to join them with my son, now my only child, who was three years old. As my parental home had been partly destroyed in air raids, and the rooms still standing were being used by the Russians as a field hospital, we went to live in our former hunting lodge. It was remote from the main roads in the middle of a large forest, with no electricity or running water, cut off from the outside world. Very little news reached us, and what did get through was unreliable. All I knew about Feri was that he had been seen in a Romanian assembly camp. He was said to have had no overcoat, and only shoes, not boots. Then his troop train had gone on eastward. Only years later was I to discover that he had been condemned to death by a Russian court martial at that time. Immediately after the Second World War, a democratic government was formed in Hungary under the protection of the victorious powers. For the first time in the history of our country, free elections were held. The initial and unanimous decision taken by the new regime was as unexpected as a natural phenomenon: the most radical imaginable agrarian reform. Large landowners had their estates expropriated, with immediate effect, and declared the property of the state. 'Large' was defined as any area of over 1000 acres, roughly equivalent to 500 hectares. The expropriation was total, and there was no compensation at all. The state immediately divided the land between those who lived on it and small farmers. It was to become the property of the working people.

From today's point of view, that may be seen as a long overdue move. But for those of us directly affected, agrarian reform was a serious blow, literally removing the ground from under our feet.

At the time, however, we couldn't grasp the real catastrophe, let alone put it into words: the reform as a whole led to the collapse of a system that had lasted for centuries. A world disappeared. Looking back today, it seems to me remarkable that neither hatred nor revenge came to the fore. Instead, the reaction was a deep, dismayed and speechless silence.

My father said nothing at all on the subject, or indeed any other. He remained silent to the day of his death where such matters were concerned, and found his few moments of happiness walking in the forest. He, my mother and all of us became moles, retreating into our burrows. We believed in nothing any more, and thought of nothing further ahead than the next few hours. It was the only way to survive.

Agnes

Next day we crawled out of our beds and walked around. We had nothing but the clothes on our backs, and our wooden clogs. 'Why do you wear shoes like that?' one of the Russians asked us, and we said, 'They are the only shoes we have.'

So they took us to the nearby town with them and drove up to a shoe shop. The shop was bolted, but that didn't keep the Russians from opening it. There was utter chaos in the town, no order at all, people on the streets everywhere, soldiers, wounded men, others coming home, refugees, inmates of the camps. Everything was disorder inside the shop as well. I found myself a pair of lace-up shoes and went out again. When the Russian who had brought me there saw me he asked, 'Is that all?' He went back into the shop, took as many pairs of shoes as he could carry, and gave them to me. 'There, now you have shoes,' he said.

With fourteen other girls, I went to ask the mayor of the town for help – we wanted to go back to Hungary and get home to our families. Two police officers said they would drive us to the Czech border in a small truck.

The people at the border didn't want to let us cross at first, and put us in quarantine. However, we were determined not to be locked up yet again, and we simply went on until we reached the university city of Brünn [Brno]. We had no luggage, and by now there were only eight of us. Russian soldiers were standing around at the railway station, and you always had to be careful with them, or one of them might grab you. We had no idea what train to board, but somehow or other we made it to Bratislava, where we saw Red Cross tents at the station. The helpers there gave us something to eat, and offered to let us rest on plank beds. But we all wanted to go on as fast as possible, and make our way home to Budapest at last.

Maritta

Hungary was in ruins. My family were scattered all over the country, and the social order was topsy-turvy. The greatest danger threatening us came not from the Soviet solders, but from the communists, who had sworn to get their revenge after the fall of the capital, and swarmed out like hornets. It would have been so easy, then as now, to blame everything on the Soviets, but it was our own people who no longer wanted us. 'Your turn now, you counts and officers who obeyed Horthy,' was the general feeling.

A single suspicion – and not always even that – was enough to get you arrested. The lie took root. The best examples of the results are the monstrous show trials. Right at the start came the trial of Cardinal Mindszenty and our close relation Prince Esterházy. The cardinal stood for the Catholic Church, the prince for a thousand years of feudal rule. We watched in helpless horror as they were humiliated and publicly condemned. Not a word of the charges was true.

The world became a distorting mirror. Only the blackest of humour could help us to bear it. Because, as reflected in that mirror, we were in the very front row. By 'we' I mean my family, our relations, our kith and kin, in short our entire social class. Until now I had been more or less free of any class consciousness at all. But now I knew who we were: aliens, the enemies of the people. We were the culprits.

Agnes

The journey took three weeks. Three weeks after the end of the war, I was home in Budapest at last. Rows of buildings lay in ruins, the trams were not running. People stood in small groups everywhere, all talking to each other. And they were saying that the first Jews were back from internment in the camps. We were something of a sensation. Many people helped us, and gave us food and clothes. The girls with whom I had been travelling hurried off to look for their families. I myself went to see my best friend, who lived near the railway station. She would be able to tell me where my parents were. Her mother opened the door. We embraced, and she began crying.

'Do you know what's happened to my parents?' I asked. 'Were they taken away?'

But she could hardly speak, and told me to ask her daughter. So I went back to the streets to look for my friend. I was running, I could hardly wait for the news.

Maritta

In the hunting lodge, far from the outside world, life went on. We built an outhouse where, as if by some miracle, we were soon keeping a pig and a few chickens. Later we had a cow too. As a result, I learned to milk, and even enjoyed it. I would sit on a low stool in the evening, my forehead resting against the cow's side, watching the interplay of my hands. I felt the movement of the animal's breathing, and drew in the aroma of fresh milk.

The local committee responsible for the distribution of land allotted my father about ten acres; barren little fields on steep slopes. They merged gently with the surrounding hilly landscape, and when the full moon stood above the valley they were a magical sight. I considered that romantic view my reward for hard labour. The fields had to be cultivated with a hoe, working uphill, row of plants after row of plants, and under the blazing sun the job seemed never-ending. When I itched because I was dripping with sweat, I gave myself a break to smoke a cigarette. Then I would sit on the stony ground, let my eyes wander, and draw the smoke in deeply.

Although Budapest was just under a hundred kilometres away, it took a whole day to reach the capital. You had to get up very early, stand by the roadside and wait for the miners' bus to come along. If you were lucky, it would take you to the nearest railway station, and at some point a train would come along. Budapest was a fascinating place at that period. The sight of the city, destroyed and yet coming back to life, was both captivating and horrible, particularly when you came there out of the forest. The worst of the rubble had not yet been cleared away, but something new was springing up everywhere, stirring, putting out new shoots, growing and proliferating. And the black market was doing well, along with barter, while dubious deals were done. Even the most naïve of plans flourished in this atmosphere, with its sense of a new beginning.

If there was a suitable room in a house – one left over when the old, the sick and small children had been accommodated – it became a salon. There were cheerful meetings every day. There had always been much drinking in Hungary, but at this time the Hungarians drank more than ever, almost impossible as that might seem.

Agnes

I ran and ran, and at last I found my friend. It was so long since I had seen her. We hugged and held hands. 'Do you know anything about my parents?' I asked. 'Were they taken away too?'

'No,' she said, shaking her head.

'Are they alive?' I asked.

'They killed themselves.'

'Suicide?'

11

The day after our arrival in Moscow, I went to the Gulag Museum with my father. It took us some time to find it; there were no signs pointing to the museum anywhere. And the passers by on the road who stopped to speak to us – most of them simply walked on – had never heard of it and shook their heads. Gulag? *Nyet.*

But we did find it, in an inner courtyard. A small building on two or three floors, a few maps on the walls, old photographs of huts in the snow, showing emaciated men in thick jackets and fur-lined boots. There was a room with a wooden plank bed in it, so that visitors could imagine how the prisoners slept, how they washed, the plates from which they ate. But it all seemed too clean, too nice, like a doll's house. Standing in front of a large map, you could press a few buttons and small lights would come on, one for each camp. The Gulag Archipelago as told to children.

Where was Stalin's power? The terror? Over two million prisoners from Germany and Austria alone had been taken prisoner and dragged away, and in addition 300,000 Hungarians, the last of whom, a man called András Toma, did not go home until the year 2000. Countless Italians, Japanese and Americans had been dispersed all over the Soviet Union, from the Polish border to Cape Dezhnev on the easternmost point of Siberia. A large number of them starved or froze to death, or were shot on the march to the camps. Many who had been through the Nazi period said that Hitler had been nothing to this. One inmate who had been in Dachau was said to have hanged himself on hearing that he was bound for

Siberia. Letters from the gulag prisoners, the *zeks*, as they were called, show that many of them wished the Americans would drop a nuclear bomb on Siberia too.

But the great majority of prisoners came from the Soviet Union itself. Under Stalin, politicians, peasants, teachers, medical doctors disappeared, and so did whole ethnic groups – Germans living in Russia – as well as children and women. In her autobiography Yevgenia Ginsburg, who was imprisoned in Siberia for eighteen years, described a group of children in the camp who were allowed to rear some puppies, but they couldn't think of names for them. The children's surroundings had robbed them of imagination. So they gave the puppies names like 'pan' and 'bucket', because those were things that they saw every day.

In his book *Travels in Siberia*, the American journalist Ian Frazier mentions an incident in the summer of 1933. A ship, the Dzhurma, with thousands of prisoners on board, came into harbour in the town of Nakhodka, near Vladivostok. At about the same time, the Chelyuskin, a research vessel, was going eastward along the Arctic coast to carry out scientific studies. Winter came unexpectedly early that year, and the Chelyuskin was caught in the ice off Chukotka. Soviet newspapers covered the event, people all over the world followed the fortunes of the scientists. The Norwegians offered to help to save the people on board the Chelyuskin, but the Soviets declined their aid. In fact they then succeeded in freeing the researchers from the ice themselves, a feat celebrated in the media as a victory. Only years later did it become clear just why the Russians had turned down any help at the time.

The ship carrying prisoners, the Dzhurma, was also stuck in the ice, only 200 miles from the Chelyuskin, but no one was to know about it. Thousands of people – prisoners, guards, sailors – had to endure months without food or any hope of rescue. No one knows what really happened in those days. It was rumoured that the crew ate the prisoners, and when the Dzhurma came to harbour next spring, there was not a single convict left among the survivors. Those who came on land, the captain and a few members of the crew, had lost their minds.

But no sense of this madness was conveyed in the museum.

I thought of a scene in Alexander Solzhenitsyn's *The Gulag Archipelago*, a book that I had brought on this journey. I planned to read it on the plane, but I had not got far, what with the small print and the many pages. Instead, I watched my father trying to open a packet of nut chocolate. He pulled and tore at it, put one end in his mouth, but nothing worked. So he put it back on the white polystyrene tray handed out to all the passengers when we were an hour into our flight, somewhere over Poland. The tray also held a small portion of chicken and mushrooms – or was it turkey?

In his book, Solzhenitsyn describes a party conference somewhere in the provinces, thousands of kilometres from Moscow, yet still not far enough away. At the end of the conference there are professions of loyalty to Stalin, and everyone stands up and applauds. They clap for three or four minutes, their hands hurt, their raised arms ache, the more elderly among those present are gasping for air, but no one dares to stop first. Six minutes pass, seven, they are all looking at one another, casting each other surreptitious glances of faint hope. In the back rows of the crowd you can pretend to be clapping and stop for a while, but not the committee at members at the front, not in front of everyone. Nine minutes go by, ten, they clap and will go on clapping until they fall over, until they are carried out on stretchers. In the eleventh minute, the manager of a paper factory drops into his chair, everyone else does the same, and the applause abruptly dies away. The spell has been broken, the other men are saved. That night the factory manager is arrested. Without more ado, and on some entirely different pretext, he is condemned to ten years in prison. And the records of the trial show that he is told, 'And in future never be the first to stop clapping.'

How can grown people clap for eleven minutes out of fear?

How do you manipulate an entire nation? There was none of that on show in this museum. And what about the hunger of which I have read so much? There are said to have been *zeks* who ate engine lubricant and roasted cats, or drank grass soup. And those who could not resist the flowers and clover growing between the huts in summer did not live long. The main cause of death in the camps was starvation; every prisoner got a piece of bread, porridge, poorly thrashed oats, and cabbage, always cabbage. Then there was the cold that I read about in the work of Varlam Shalamov, a Russian writer who had spent, in all, seventeen years in the camps; old lags could tell almost exactly how cold it was, even without a thermometer. When there was freezing fog, it was minus forty degrees outside; when you breathed out noisily but breathing itself wasn't difficult yet, it was minus forty-five; when you breathed noisily and you were also short of breath, it was fifty degrees below zero. At more than minus fifty degrees below zero, your saliva froze in the air.

There was nothing to be learnt about all this in the rooms of the Gulag Museum, but above all, it never tackled the question of why so little about it is known today. The life of prisoners of war in the former Soviet Union is 'the most neglected subject of contemporary history,' said one of the books I had read in preparation for this journey. Why has hardly anything been written about it? Why are there hardly any films? Why is the Gulag Museum hidden away in a back yard in Moscow? And why is it so small, housing so few exhibits?

There isn't even agreement on the number of victims of Stalinism. Sixty million Russians are said to have died of causes other than natural death under the entire period of communist dictatorship from 1917 to 1992. A great many of those under the rule of Stalin, small images of whom could be bought in Moscow's tobacconist shops, as car stickers, doll-sized figures to stand on your shelf at home, a card game featuring the highest-ranking communists, all of them criminals: Stalin was the ace of spades.

*

Very, very many books about the Shoah say that such things must never happen again; that is why they were written. Hence all the memorial occasions, the exhibitions, films, studies, archives, even fifty, sixty, seventy years after the Holocaust. So why does that not apply to the horrors of Russian communist rule? Why, I asked myself, looking into the eyes of Lenin's photograph on the wall, why don't they bother anyone?

My father sat down on a folding chair in a corner. Was he tired again? Or had the photos on the walls, the plank bed, the reproduction of a dungeon cell taken more out of him than I'd thought? I put my hand on his shoulder; that seemed to do him good.

We were accompanied on our tour of the museum by Nadya, a young woman in her mid-thirties. She was curator of the exhibition, and also sold tickets as you came in and served in the cafetria. She seemed to be responsible for the history of the Stalinist terror all on her own, a small, delicate woman with thin hair. We asked her a few questions. Had any prisoners ever managed to escape? 'What was it like when they were allowed to go home?' I asked. 'Home to their families – did they talk about what they had been through?'

Nadya looked at us as if she could have told us a great deal about the silence of all those men, lasting to this day, about life after the camp on the 21st floor of a grey tower block on the outskirts of a bleak city. But her English, she said, wasn't good enough. She shook her head, shrugged, compressed her lips. She wanted to talk, but it was no use. However, when my father was saying goodbye to her, and told her, in English, 'My father, ten years, gulag,' her awkwardness suddenly disappeared. 'I'm so sorry,' she replied, also in English, taking his hands in hers and looking into his eyes for a long time. They stood like that for what seemed to me like several minutes, without any need for words, as he fought back tears.

We went to Red Square on the underground railway. To reach it, you have to brace your full weight against metal swing doors as if you wanted to jostle someone on purpose. 'Why is Moscow full of such infernal devices?' asked my father, as he stood in front of them incredulously and also afraid, as old people sometimes stand looking at escalators. I glanced at him. 'Oh, do come on,' I told him. Why was I so impatient with him? Because I couldn't stand the exhibition, and the fact that he was too weak for all this. I couldn't stand his fragility, that was it.

'Russia was . . .' he began.

'Like Auschwitz. I know . . .'

'Don't say it like that. Russia was the devil, do you understand? They took everything from us. They raped a hundred thousand Hungarian women, did you know that?'

He was still standing in front of those doors, looking at other people flinging themselves heavily against them. A few women in leather boots, on the other hand, waited for the moment when the doors swung outward again, and then quickly slipped through. 'The Russians drank methyl alcohol out of petroleum lamps, can you imagine that? The Germans were more civilized.'

'The Nazis? Civilized?' I asked. 'You can't mean that seriously.'

'Not every German was a Nazi,' he replied. Then I took his arm and hauled him through the doorway, just as I make my son go into the bathroom when he doesn't want me to brush his teeth. We went along a passage, past stout women selling jars of horseradish. I was still holding my father's coat. We passed cabbages lying on the ground in cartons, socks, fake Gucci belts, and he let me guide him. Hadn't it once been the other way around? Yes, surely there had been a time when he was the one who saw me safely over the road, and kept my ID in his jacket pocket for me. At some point, however, we had switched roles. Now it was I who led him down underground railway passages, pointed out puddles to him, and made sure that he didn't bump into anything. When exactly did that change happen, the one that every son silently experiences with his father? Was it a particular day? A particular moment? And did both of us accept it?

After a long search, we decided on a Japanese restaurant where the sushi came rattling past on a conveyor belt. It was late afternoon, and darkness had fallen some time ago. We drank vodka and talked about my grandfather, not during his time in the camp but before that, when he had been a soldier in the Hungarian army, fighting beside the Germans first in Poland, then in Ukraine.

'Did he shoot people?' I asked my father as I dissolved wasabi in soy sauce.

'Never.'

'How can you be in the army without shooting?'

'He wouldn't have hurt a fly. And he was very religious.'

'So?'

'So – what?'

'This tastes good. How is yours?'

'Not so bad. I don't want chopsticks. Do they have forks here?'

'Did Hungarian soldiers have to give the Hitler salute?'

'Oh, I don't know.'

'After all, Hungary was Germany's most loyal ally.'

'Are you trying to tell me your grandfather was a Nazi?'

Of course this conversation ended in a quarrel. Hitler, the gulag, religion and vodka – it was all too much for us. I got angrier by the minute, louder, and more drunk, because as usual I felt I couldn't get close to him. I could have stripped naked, jumped up on the conveyor belt, I could have danced and shouted, and he still wouldn't have noticed. Everything slid off him: water off a duck's back . I told him I was seeing a psychoanalyst twice a week, because I thought that might entice him out of his reserve; I told him that I asked myself questions about my background, my identity . 'I often feel as if I'm not there, if you see what I mean.' But he didn't. He could never tell what was going on inside me, not when I was a child, not now, and it infuriated me. My words simply did not get through. I saw them slide away from him like wet snow running down a window pane, collecting in puddles of useless slush on the ground. Then I stood up and shook him, while raw fish travelled past us.

I don't know why I did that. I had been in a few fights at school, and once in a bar in the evening, but I'd never been particularly strong, and I was not used to physical violence. But now I grabbed his red sweater with the zip fastener, the one that his new wife had given him for his birthday; my parents had divorced when I was fifteen years old. I didn't hit him, but I was close to it – and he didn't defend himself. He didn't push me away, or shout at me; my father was ready to give in. So we stood there for a few seconds, while I did not look him in the eyes but stared at the metal frame of his glasses, and forgot everything else around me: the customers at the next table, sushi, Moscow, the gulag. After a while I let go of him and sat down. I felt exhausted.

'It's the vodka,' he said after a while, straightening his sweater.

'It's the vodka,' I agreed, full of shame, hearing my pulse thumping against my skull. I took one of his cigarettes and lit it, although I hadn't smoked for years. I didn't have the courage to look up from the table top until my phone buzzed: a text from my wife: 'Children ill, tonsilitis.'

'That's all we needed,' he said when I read out the message, and shook his head. 'What do we do now?'

What did we do now? I didn't know. You're the father, I thought, you ought to know what to do.

Taxis were so expensive that we went back through those swing doors, past the cabbages, the horseradish, men with toothpicks in the corners of their mouths selling batteries, and took the underground back to our hotel. We said nothing until we were in our room on the fourteenth floor of that ugly tower building in the ugly city where I had nearly broken my father's nose. He put his pyjamas on; I was in my underpants when we embraced without a word.

*

I woke up and found that my sense of shame had not gone away overnight. We dressed, breakfasted, and set out. We had an engagement to meet Dimitri Petrov, and acted as if nothing had happened yesterday. Petrov is the director of an organization called Memorial that has been working on the communist dictatorship since the late eighties. Like Yad Vashem in Jerusalem, its aim is to publish the names and biographical details of all victims of the regime. Petrov was sitting in his little office, books everywhere, cartons full of leaflets. They knew nothing about Stalin in Russia, he said, and very little was told to schoolchildren. There were even attempts to rehabilitate him, and a few provincial madmen wanted to put up an obelisk in his memory. Petrov laughed, his long grey hair falling over his face. 'It's all worse under Putin.' Yeltsin had allowed access to the archives, but since Putin came to power silence had been imposed again. 'We're not like the Germans, we don't analyse the past, admit to mistakes and recognize our guilt. Here we say: so there were camps, there was the gulag, Stalin had his bad side, but above all he won, he won great victories and brought us economic progress. The heroic moments of Russian history take precedence over its dark chapters.'

A few years ago, Petrov's organization had drawn up a list of demands to help people come to terms with the past. It wanted to see the archives of the secret service opened, and Stalin's reign of terror properly assessed in school textbooks. It was asking for a monument like the Holocaust Memorial in Berlin, and a museum complex for students and historians. Medvedev, who was president at the time, said he would certainly see to the matter soon. But nothing happened.

Petrov leafed through the file on my grandfather that I had given him. Not much light came into his office through the window. He read the wording of the death sentence passed on my grandfather, read about his transfer from Voronezh to Stalingrad, and from there to Asbest. Cars rushed by outside; my father was sitting beside me. I could sense that he liked Petrov. He laughed, cracked jokes, it was so much easier for him to talk about Communism and the gulag than about himself, I thought. He asked questions, quoted from books, showed his curiosity. Only when the subject turned to us, to my mother, to me, did he become tired and monosyllabic. Was that what distinguished my generation from his and Petrov's? The fact that we have never experienced an outside foreign power changing everything, when there was nothing an individual could do about it? We lacked that experience, the recognition that we were powerless, not the centre of the world, and the experience of having to see judgement passed on us from outside. Instead, we were experts on our own ego, we could discuss our personal relationships for nights on end, talk about our sexual preferences and our gluten allergies. Did we look in at ourselves too much, while they only looked out?

*

Now my father and Petrov were talking about Mátyás Rákosi, son of a Jewish businessman, who had been in power in Hungary in the fifties. Many of the communists who held high office, like the party leaders Ernő Gerő and József Révai, and Gábor Péter the founder of the political police, were Jews. The anti-Semitism so prevalent in Hungary today can be ascribed, among other things, to that fact. The main argument of the anti-Semites, as we hear it at demonstrations of the Hungarian ruling party and read it on Internet forums, is that the Jews not only controlled the banks and the media, but after the war had been model communists – which is regarded as one of the ugliest of all epithets today.

'Rákosi was one of the worst criminals in history,' I heard my father say to Petrov. 'A dictator who makes Gaddafi look like a schoolboy.' And once again I felt anger rise in me as it had in the Japanese restaurant the day before. What was I actually doing here? Why was I here at all? I had prepared well for this journey, I had read my grandfather's file, Shalamov's accounts of life in the camps,

Baberovski's biography of Stalin, but now it felt as if I had been deluding myself.

Hadn't I flown to Siberia to get my father to notice me at long last? And now that we were here, I had to accept that he couldn't notice me because there was so much in the way, hiding his view of me: communism, the gulag, Rákosi, our forebears in their uniforms, the men with swords, the women with billowing skirts. They all came pushing in between us, and Lenin too stood somewhere or other, smiling. No wonder my father couldn't see me. But it was Stalin who drew most attention to himself. He waved his hands about, he twirled the ends of his mighty moustache. 'You'll never drive me away,' he shouted at me, and I saw his yellow teeth. I could fall off high walls, as I did in my childhood; I could dye my hair, as I did in my teens; I could shake my father as I had shaken him yesterday, but Stalin was right. I had no chance of getting close to my father, not compared to him.

I remembered a phone conversation with my father a few weeks before our visit to Siberia. He said that they had been showing films all day about the 1956 rising, when Hungary rebelled against the communists. That day is now celebrated every year, with parades, memorial events, lectures, people laying wreaths and lighting candles. 'The popular revolution,' he told me, 'was really the most important event in my life.' He had spent all that day in his living-room at home feeling melancholy, he added. 'I was weeping inside. You don't understand me.'

'Of course I understand you,' I had replied, and I showed my concern for him. 'Are you feeling better now?'

Here in Petrov's office, however, I really didn't understand. If the 1956 uprising had been the most important event in his life, where did that leave me? And where did it leave my brothers? Did we come fourth? Or fifth? Or did we slip right out of his top ten, as tennis players slip out of the top ratings in a bad year? Did we come before the seizure of power by the communists in 1948, or just after the bombing of Budapest? Were we in contention for third place with his emigration to Switzerland?

*

Petrov went on looking through the files. 'Such a shame,' he kept saying. For a while my grandfather had worked as a paramedic for a German doctor; he had been a male nurse for a long time, said the files. 'He tried escaping in the autumn of 1953.' He read the passage aloud to us, edict number 97, Camp 84, section 2: my grandfather had been caught planning his flight, and as a punishment had to spend a whole month in the cells. It was in the same year as Stalin died and Khrushchev became party secretary. Many foreign prisoners of war had been set free at the time, but my grandfather was not among them. Petrov explained, 'Anyone who could show the camp administrators that he was a good communist, read Marx and participated in the Antifa [anti-Fascist] courses could hope to be discharged early.' But that obviously did not include my grandfather, whom Petrov called Feri, as if they had been friends. 'Feri spent a lot of time in the cells in those last years.' Petrov leafed through the monthly records: November 1953, February 1954, when Mátyás Rákosi, that mini-Stalin, had already lost power; Khrushchev favoured the more moderate Imre Nagy. The chancellors of Germany and Austria, Konrad Adenauer and Julius Raab, exerted political pressure to get the last prisoners freed at last. Hence the event recorded in document number 03-1875446, and dated 20 November 1955: 'The case of the prisoner of war Batthyány, born 1915 in Kittsee, is closed.'

In the last weeks before his repatriation, he was fattened up with bread, sausage and soup. No one at home was to see the wretched state in which he had spent the last ten years. Even on the way back in the train, he had the theses of Marx and Engels dinned into him, in the hope that he would prove to be a good socialist at home. My grandfather reached the Hungarian-Ukrainian border at Sighetu MarmaÐiei. 20,000 Jews had been deported from here to Auschwitz ten years earlier, now there were a few Red Cross tents. Those coming home from Russia, like divers, were not brought straight to the surface, but were to rest first, recover from stress, eat and sleep. During the Christmas holidays of 1955, Feri sent my grandmother a telegram: 'Arriving mid-day tomorrow if I don't die of excitement.'

At the time my father was fourteen years old, and had never seen his father except in a few photographs. He watched his mother cleaning the little apartment while a pan of meat broth simmered on top of the stove. He waited all afternoon for the metallic sound of the garden gate opening, and when it was already dark, and he was so tired that he was almost falling asleep at the table, a man in uniform with a rucksack on his back was suddenly standing in front of him.

'Do you know who I am?' the strange soldier asked him – a man with no hair left, with bad teeth, a man who would show signs of dementia early, and whose feet would feel cold until the day he died.

My father nodded.

*

A few months after my grandfather's return from Siberia, in the midst of the confusion of the popular rising of 1956, he left Hungary with his wife and child, went first to Aunt Margit and Uncle Ivan at the Villa Mita in Lugano, and from there to the Rhineland, where he was manager with power of attorney to the Thyssen Works. In the sixties and seventies, he still used to meet a remarkably large number of his former fellow prisoners. They called these frequent reunions 'discussion of the camps'. They ate cakes and drank beer and wine somewhere in Germany; their children played cowboys and Indians, their wives smoked. And the men conferred. 'Do you remember having to quarry asbestos out of the rock when the temperature was minus thirty degrees?' they whispered to one another. They sat on plastic garden chairs printed in bright colours, the TV was on in the living room, and Gerd Müller scored for Bayern München every Saturday. 'Can you remember how we ate soap to make ourselves seem feverish?'

But my grandfather soon showed signs of boredom. He hid his yawns, like a well-behaved child. 'Hey, Feri, do you remember?' No, not in great detail any more. The details were blurred, he couldn't remember place names. But his comrades of the camps, former Wehrmacht soldiers – who knew what they had done for Hitler in the war? – took it badly when he came to such gatherings less and less often, and at some point stopped coming at all. 'Hey, Feri, where've you been?'

Their feelings were injured, as if by a new kind of war wound, to find one of them leaving the dance, no longer wanting to remember – or able to do so. Until my grandfather lost his memory entirely, until his everyday life, consisting of details repeated daily – crispbread for breakfast, a bath, a walk to the park – pushed its way in, hiding the images of the old days.

A letter came one morning. He opened it slowly, picked up his magnifying glass, read and read, and shook his bald head. He could make nothing of either the signature or what the letter said. It began with the words, 'Do you still remember a young Soviet lieutenant?' It was the Russian of the past, Efim Etkind, who had made him his interpreter. He wrote to say that he had been looking out for him for years, and now, by chance, had come upon his address. Could they meet? And so a few weeks later they sat facing one another, two elderly gentlemen brought together by international history.

'Who are you?' my grandfather asked him.

'Efim Etkind.'

'But you still have plenty of hair.'

'Well, yes – by comparison with an egg.'

A few months later my grandfather was dead.

12

That afternoon we flew from Moscow to Yekaterinburg, where we spent four days searching for anything that remained of the camps. We had a ramshackle yellow minibus, a driver who looked like the Chinese artist Ai Weiwei, and a humourless interpreter called Svetlana who accompanied us on our tour. Over the last few years, she told us, more and more visitors had come to this region: Italians, Finns, Japanese. 'They want to know what life here was like for their fathers and grandfathers.' Snow lay on the ground outside, not metres deep but enough to cover everything. 'It is quite mild for the time of year, minus fifteen degrees,' said Svetlana. 'There are days when it's difficult to breathe because the cold air hurts your lungs.'

Yekaterinburg is in the Ural Mountains that divide Europe from Asia. It is 8,500 kilometres from there to the other end of Siberia, Magadan on the Sea of Okhotsk. In between lie tundra, Lake Baikal, and steppes that seem endless, full of gnats in summer and under the permafrost in winter.

We drove into a small town called Revda, where my grandfather had spent a few months in captivity in 1951. 'There's not much to see in this place,' Svetlana told us. She had been here once before with a couple of Germans. Only in the north of Siberia, in the middle of the forest, did a few former watchtowers and the remains of barbed wire still stand. 'As if human beings had been living there a few weeks earlier,' I read in an account by someone who had walked through the snow for days until he came upon huts and original helmets. The Siberian snow preserved everything, this author wrote. Even the atmosphere of the time was still perceptible.

However, our yellow bus stopped not at any watchtowers but outside a poultry farm surrounded by a wooden fence, and when we got out we sank ankle-deep into the slush. 'Your grandfather was somewhere here too,' Svetlana told me.

'Here?'

Had we come thousands of kilometres to stand beside this fence? My father coughed, and looked for his cigarettes. He had been smoking again since we landed in Moscow. He felt nervous, he had told me after coming out of a tobacconist's with a few packets of Marlboros. That cough, the slight rattle in his throat that I heard now while the acrid smell of chickens rose to my nostrils, reminded me of my childhood: the packet of Marlboros in his shirt pocket under his sweater, the sound as he removed the silver paper. I looked at the farm, and pictured thousands of undernourished chickens in there, sitting on perches covered with droppings and pecking out each other's feathers, while they joylessly laid small eggs to end up in the frying pans of people who lived on the seventh floor of concrete apartment blocks without any balconies.

Once again it struck me as strange that there were no memorial tablets anywhere, nothing indicating what had happened here in the past. Today people live and work, have children and get married and keep chickens, where prisoners were once exploited and murdered. The connection between the past and the future has always fascinated me. Wasn't that what I missed so much in Switzerland? The fact that streets, houses, town districts told no stories because nothing much ever changed, and when it did it was only for the better? Didn't those years of stability and security, so much vaunted by all the Swiss, also blunt the mind a little? If the only movement is onward and upward, isn't some depth of focus missing?

I always particularly liked those brass plates in the entrances of buildings in Vienna and Budapest that summarize, in a few words, what had happened there in the past, who had lived and who had died in them. I was addicted to the little thrill that those words gave me, the idea that many years ago there had been a field hospital or a torture chamber in what is a school today. Wasn't a building something like a section through time? A soil sample showing various sedimentary rocks stacked on top of each other, each stratum providing evidence of past conditions?

'Let's get back in the bus,' said my father, and Ai Weiwei started the engine. But I stayed where I was for a little longer, because I couldn't take my eyes off that camp for chickens. Maybe a man would come out with empty feeding troughs, wondering what we were here for. Maybe that man's name was Simanovsky, and he was the son of my grandfather's former warder, the major who took his temperature and kept sending him back to the cells. Why not? A camp for humans, a camp for chickens – it could run in the family. Only when Ai Weiwei hooted, and gestured to me to get in, did I tear myself away.

We went to Asbest on our last day. Vladimir Motrevich, a university professor in Yekaterinburg, went with us. For many years he has been studying the penal camps that stood in this district, the Oblast Sverdlovsk, about a hundred of them. Motrevich regularly carried out exhumations, salvaged graves, looked for traces of the past. The Hungarians, he said, had been the toughest of the prisoners, more used to cold than, for instance, Italians. Motrevich told us about the famine of the postwar years from 1946 to 1949. 'Prisoners in the camps were often better off than the local inhabitants.' He was not especially popular hereabouts, said the professor, because everyone wanted to forget what had happened, and here was he bringing history back to the surface again. 'There were cases of cannibalism,' he said in Russian, and Svetlana translated what he said while our yellow bus made its way along icy roads through the snow-covered landscape. 'Professor Motrevich says that children were regularly eaten.' Even before she had time to take in what she had just said, the professor was going on, telling us that thousands had committed suicide, and I looked at my father. 'Where have we ended up?'

'Didn't I tell you we were in hell?'

Svetlana, noticing our astonishment, said, 'Circumstances were tragic in the past. Of course it is different today. You can go for wonderful bicycle rides in summer.'

'In what summer?' I asked.

Motrevich laughed when he saw our faces. He was wearing a large fur cap, the kind that suits only Russians, and when he took it off now it deprived him of some of his imposing aura. Svetlana had launched into paeans of praise for the countryside, nature, the local food. 'And there's also an orchestra,' she said. The bus passed forests of leafless trees, factories with gigantic pipes winding their way around the buildings like snakes. 'And good universities,' Svetlana went on, as we went into a slight skid on an old railway level crossing.

Most of the 70,000 people of Asbest make their living in the mine. It is a mono-culture, like so many in Russia, with everyone working for the same firm. If Ural-Asbest closed, thousands of people would lose their livelihood. There is no town centre, only a few streets, all the factory buildings, and then the largest open asbestos mine in the world — eleven kilometres long, three hundred metres deep, a crater in which diggers and cranes stand, scraping at that gigantic wound and daily bringing out new material to be sold to China and India (asbestos is banned in Europe now), where the fibres settle in the pulmonary alveoli of human beings, forming small lumps over the months and years.

The people of Asbest talked about the dust that covered everything: window panes, the freshly washed linen that they hung out in the garden to dry, blackberries – and they complained of a painful cough that wouldn't go away. Asbestos is known to this day as 'the white needles'. One pensioner whom we talked to remembered, 'It was often so dusty in the air of the factories that you couldn't see your own hands.' Another talked about his lung trouble; he had never smoked, but leaving this place had never crossed his mind. Where would he go?

My grandfather came here in the late summer of 1953. It was on his prison record that he complained of psychological problems. 'My nerves are shattered. I feel weak and ill. In my condition, any kind of work would mean my death. I feel that I am destroying myself. I need to recuperate.' No one took any notice of that. The prisoner was capable of working, said the record. He was given clothing suitable for the time of year and taken to the mine. The file does not say exactly what work he did there. Professor Motrevich told us that everything now carried out by machines was done at that time by prisoners of war, and many of them died as a result of their work and the hard conditions.

He had found several cemeteries in the vicinity of Asbest, he said, including the grave of six Wehrmacht generals. The administrations of the camps where they died recorded the deaths meticulously, and wrote accounts that ended up in the archives of the Ministry of the Interior, marked 'Strictly secret.' In the nineties, when the inhabitants of Asbest found out how many people had died there, they couldn't believe it, said Motrevich, who had put his cap on again. It upset them. How, they had wondered, was that possible? And all before their own eyes? Like the people of Rechnitz, the older ones anyway, who claimed to have seen nothing to do with the slaughter of the Jews, the Siberians were astonished when they found out what had happened here in broad daylight, while they sat in their own little homes.

And how, I asked myself, can people be so blind? How can a whole nation not want to look? But is it so much better today?

*

According to his file, my grandfather had made another attempt to escape in the winter of 1953. He had been caught packing bread and sausage in his rucksack; he didn't confess, but everything pointed to his guilt, wrote the same Major Simanovsky I already knew from the records. I read the passage aloud to my father. I was glad to know that Feri had tried to run for it. Several documents are evidence of his attempts to convince the administration of the camp that he was not a Hungarian but an Austrian. Most of his family's property, he wrote, was in what is now Austrian territory. As an Austrian, he hoped to get better treatment and go home earlier, but his requests were refused. That seems to have radicalized him. He stole food not just for himself but also for others, say the files in April 1954. He complained of poor clothing in May 1954, and refused to work on a Sunday. 'I am a Catholic, and in my religion Sunday is a day of rest.' From the winter of 1954 he was in one of the cells nearly all the time, an unheated, cramped room without natural daylight, as Motrevich told us. 'The prisoner Batthyány' (this was written not by Simanovsky but by a man called Kuznetzov) 'worked badly and did not fulfil his norm. 'He is a bad influence on the rest of his brigade.'

'Isn't that wonderful?' I said to my father. 'He was resisting. He defended himself instead of just accepting everything. He wasn't a moral coward.'

'What do you think was wonderful about those years?' my father retorted. He sat in silence in our vehicle for the rest of the morning, exchanging civil remarks with Svetlana, but most of the time he just looked out of the window without moving.

We visited a dilapidated housing estate on the outskirts of Asbest. The professor knew a former nurse, now over ninety years old, who had looked after the prisoners of war. Tatiana Vodamonia took out her magnifying glass with hands that shook, and held it over the two photos of my grandfather from the files. We were in her small apartment. Suppose she recognized him? Suppose she had treated him? Or worked beside him – hadn't he acted as a paramedic here?

She looked first at the photo showing him as a healthy young man in 1945. Then the other one, the picture of a sick man, an inmate of the camp. 'I feel that I am destroying myself,' he had written. I couldn't get that remark from his records out of my head.

But Tatiana didn't recognize him. Instead, she talked about companies of total strangers, emaciated, desperate men. The women in the village were sorry for them, but what could they do? They were hungry themselves, most of them were on their own; their husbands had died at Stalingrad or in some other battle.

'They had to work for twelve hours a day,' said Tatiana, but the cold had been the worst of it. 'There were small wood-burning stoves in the huts, but they warmed only those sitting right next to them.' The prisoners made themselves little paraffin lamps, called *kolymka*, out of food cans. They gave a little light and made the air smell foul. 'It was so cold in their beds that in the morning their hair was frozen to the pillows.' She talked about the few affairs between prisoners of war and Russian women. Some of the Germans had stayed on after they were freed, had raised families and worked for Ural-Asbest of their own free will.

We drove back through the snow that afternoon. Motrevich had some old plans of the camps with him, and pointed out of the window. 'Somewhere here was Camp Number 84, close to the rails.' I had my grandfather's file on my knees in front of me, photocopies of the interrogations, plans, medical records. I remembered a place where it said that my grandfather had hurt his hand during 'construction of the tracks'. 'Wait a moment,' I said, and Ai Weiwei stopped. Our yellow bus was in the middle of the road with its windscreen wipers on, making a sound like the wheezing of a tired old horse as they swept from side to side. The windows were clouded, and when we wiped the condensation away with our sleeves we saw a small birch wood, deep snow, no trace of any huts, cells or watchtowers. To my surprise, my father, who had seemed so tired all day, got up, pushed the sliding door open with a jerk, and went out into the cold.

'Where are you going?'

'Isn't this what we came for?'

'Suppose we're wrong?' But he was already going down a slight slope; he slipped, picked himself up without knocking the snow off his trousers. I followed, expecting him to turn back soon, what with the branches hitting him in the face, the snow on his feet and the cold wind. He'll start cursing any moment now, I thought, he'll get back into the bus, he won't stand up to this for as much as two minutes. Instead, however, he kept going, past young trees and on into the void. 'He was here,' said my father, and something in his expression changed. His eyes were wider. I saw something like childish pleasure around his mouth. Straight-backed, he trudged through the snow, suddenly seeming less introverted than before. I don't know when I had last seen him like that.

We found a broken iron post stuck in the ground, rusting. I was about to go back to the bus when he asked, 'Suppose this was the latrine?'

'The latrine?' I repeated. 'You think we've found his latrine?'

He nodded, and looked at me, so full of life.

Now I was the one who felt withdrawn and cold, while my father was already holding another object, part of an old tree stump. He was examining it as if he were an expert on wood. 'This must be over seventy years old. Suppose he touched that tree?' And he stowed the piece of wood in his jacket pocket; I could hardly believe it. 'I'll put it on my bedside table,' he said, and I nodded, feeling as useless as I had felt in Petrov's office not long before. I was at a loss. So I picked up a piece of a branch as well, but that felt wrong. Meanwhile my father was thinking up new ideas, climbing small mounds, looking at the view from them, finding something interesting behind every tree. 'Some kind of memorial ought to be put up,' he said. I was thinking of my toes, which were so cold that I could hardly feel them, but he couldn't get enough of this birch wood in the snow.

We had been there for about half an hour when the magic left his face, his body relaxed. It was like the effect of drugs wearing off. In silence, we went back to the bus, where Svetlana, Ai Weiwei and the professor were waiting for us.

Darkness soon fell, and my father went to sleep even before we reached the expressway. He had his hands between his legs, and looked like a child. The anger that had been my companion all these days was gone. I had never seen him look so much alive, so curious, in all our time together. Not at the birth of my children, or at my wedding. This forest, the latrine, the piece of wood in his jacket pocket were more of a release than anything I had ever done.

I had travelled to Siberia to understand that I was no match for international history, for all those wars that haunted his mind. So I was not angry and did not shout at him any more; no, it was worse. Stalin, I whispered to myself, first robbed all your family of its land, then locked your grandfather up, and after that took your father away from you.

We flew back next day. The sun was shining, and ice crystals sparkled on the windows of our bus on the way to the airport. Svetlana, saying goodbye, said we should come back in summer when everything was in flower, and we promised that we would, but we knew we would never set eyes on Asbest again. We still had two days to spend in Moscow, and it felt as if we were back from the wilderness, as if there was nothing that could shake us now. By mid-day we were drinking vodka and smoking like Russians, and we easily pushed open the swing doors that had been such a problem some days before. We didn't quarrel, we talked about this and that – and for once were not magnets any more. Then we flew to Munich, where we changed planes to fly home, he to Budapest, I to Zürich.

Diaries V

Agnes

When I was first back in Budapest I spent the nights in a refugee camp. People who, like me, didn't know where else to go assembled there. People who were looking for their old life and couldn't find it. After a while I even began working at the camp, distributing blankets. Having something to do was good for me, but then I fell ill with hepatitis. I was on my own, with no one to look after me. I was taken to hospital, where they nursed me and I soon got better, but still I did not feel really well. One day a nurse came along and said, 'I know what you need. You feel lonely, you have no one to talk to. Look at that man in the corridor. He's a Pole, he was in Auschwitz like you. He's here because he had water on his lungs, and he's on his own as well. Maybe it would do you good to talk to him?' The Pole with water on his lungs was to be my husband.

We spent a great deal of time together. He was a convinced Zionist, and helped people to travel on to Palestine; the state of Israel didn't exist yet. He often had to leave the city for several days, but he always came back. He had five brothers and a sister-in-law; all the other members of his family had died in the concentration camps, including his wife and child. He wanted to go to Israel with me and begin a new life there, but I was not so sure. I did know that my parents were dead, but was I to leave Hungary for ever, just like that? Who knew, perhaps there was someone who knew more about them after all, someone who could tell me just how they had died. So

I went hither and thither, in search of I didn't know exactly what, and I was afraid of losing my mind. But in the end I decided to go with my Pole, and a rabbi whom I knew from the old days married us.

Leaving Hungary was not so simple, because by now the country was occupied by the Russians. We got forged papers and went first to Fiume,* then to Milan, and from there to a little village near Turin where the rest of his family were waiting for us in an old palazzo. We were free, yet everything felt so uncertain.

Maritta

Goga was getting weaker and weaker. One night I gave her a sleeping tablet to soothe her pain, and to my horror found that she was unconscious next morning. Our supervisor put hay in his farm cart and harnessed two decrepit oxen to it. The nearest hospital was nine kilometres away. We lifted the dying woman into this provisional cradle and set out. Up and down along the stony, bumpy road, up and down as Goga was jolted about on her way into eternal life. With her, my old world lost its last beacon.

Soon after that, we had to move again because the communists were taking our hunting lodge too, after we had settled so well into it. They sent us to a little village at the back of beyond. We lived separately on two farms, my parents sharing two rooms with the farming family. My mother, of all people, slept in the kitchen. I and my son moved into a room with a family who did not particularly like us. It felt like prison, and indeed it was.

Of course it wasn't to be compared to my husband's captivity, but all the same we had been deprived of any prospects. Only the forest offered us shelter and comfort and firewood. The state-

* Translator's note: Then within the borders of Italy: now the Croatian city of Rijeka.

119

appointed forester employed us as day labourers. A few years ago, all the land here had still been ours.

Agnes

We lived in that Italian village for some time. Preparations for the rest of our journey had ground to a halt. Then one day, out of the blue, I had a telegram from the Red Cross telling me that my brother had survived. I was beside myself with joy. 'I'm not going anywhere without knowing what's going to happen to my brother,' I said. So our ways parted again; the rest of my husband's family set off for Palestine, we stayed where we were. But life wasn't easy in Italy either. There was high unemployment, and the police were intrusive, always turning up and wanting to know what we were doing. Three years passed like this. In the end we got tired of waiting, and we couldn't persuade my brother to come with us. We went to the Argentinian consulate, where they made out visas for us, and a little later we boarded a ship bound for South America.

My husband had an aunt in Buenos Aires, and she took us in. We had nothing with us apart from a few clothes, the photo of my parents from the old margarine box, and the belt that my husband had taken from a warder at Auschwitz on the day when the camp was liberated. We took a taxi in Buenos Aires, and suddenly we were in the middle of the city. This was in the year 1948.

My brother didn't want to follow us. He married and spent the rest of his life in Hungary. He had an important position in the communist civil service, he never said a word to his wife and children about his time in the concentration camp, and he died early at the age of 49.

Maritta

That was what life was like for me in that village at the back of beyond: working in the forest, my son, occasional walks and supper with my parents. There was no more to it. My mother had always been morose in the past, and now she hardly spoke; my father was silent, and I'm not known for being the life and soul of the party, so we were a rather melancholy company. We were all withdrawn. Only occasionally did we venture to go out in the fresh air and taste life. That could mean conversations, walks when, for a few moments, everything was as it had been before the war. But then we immediately withdrew, ashamed of our frivolity, and became the moles that we were from then on.

I remember one evening when I came home late. It was cold, and my son was already asleep. Since I had hardly any firewood, I put some branches I had found outside the house on the fire, and the smell immediately reminded me of the old days, of hunting parties, rum, the women's powder compacts. I took paper and a pen and set about writing it all down, every detail. I was worn out and the sun was rising when I read what I had written, and threw every separate sheet of paper on the dying embers, because after all there was no point in it. That was in 1955. I hadn't seen my husband for over ten years, and my child had grown into a gangling boy.

In that space of time I had lost everything that was once mine: my house, my home, my country. I had resigned myself to the idea that it would all end here, in this little village. But then a miracle happened: a telegram arrived from Feri, saying that he was coming home, and a year later, after the failure of the uprising against the Russians in November 1956, the three of us left Hungary. When I was allowed back again years later, I saw that nothing of the past was left. The world of my childhood lay buried under the concrete rubble of the East or the garbage of the West. Lost and gone for ever. Somewhere beyond a forgotten curve in the road.

Agnes

Seventeen years after our arrival in Buenos Aires, we travelled back to Hungary for the first time. It took all our savings to pay for the flight. All those years, the thought of my parents had haunted me. I always wanted to know how and where exactly they had died, but it was a long time before I knew the answer. On my eightieth birthday, long after my husband's death, my daughters asked what I would like as a present, and I told them I wanted to go back and see my village in Hungary once again. In preparation for the journey I began looking through all the available papers, books and documents. Maybe I might yet find a clue there?

I read that 300 Jews from the neighbouring villages had been crammed into a ghetto, including my parents, and I told my daughters, 'Let's not go to Sárosd but to where the ghetto was, in another village, quite close to it, called Sárbogárd.' When we got there, we went into the village hall to ask what had happened to the Jews in 1944. A young woman went down to the archives for us and brought the old books up. Suddenly we saw our name and the date: 1 July 1944. My father took his own life at five in the morning. My mother killed herself on the same day at eleven in the evening. They drank poison. My father was 47 years old when he died, my mother was 44.

Later that day, we went to the Jewish cemetery. We looked for their grave, but we couldn't find it. Then I noticed an old stone without any inscription or date. 'Let's use that,' I said to my daughters. 'My parents are buried here and we have found their grave.' And when we were all standing in front of the stone, taking photos, I said, 'So now let's go away. I never want to come back here again.'

13

The summer after that visit to Siberia, I took a few weeks' unpaid holiday. A friend of mine was flying to Canada, and lent me his apartment as a place where I could sleep and write. 'Do whatever it is you're planning,' he said, handing me his keys. So there I was all of a sudden in rooms new to me. The floor creaked when I walked across it, and when I stood still it was incredibly quiet, no children shouting, no phone calls and deadlines – it was like being in another life. There are some people who go to lonely forest huts to switch off from the world; I did it in a two-roomed apartment in the red light quarter of Zürich – and only until late afternoon. Then I rode my bicycle back to my children and my wife, made pasta, scraped remnants of dried-on toothpaste out of the washbasin, trod on the two rubber dinosaurs on the floor at night when one of the children was crying, and I went to see what the matter was.

But for the first time in years I was free for the rest of the day. I was finally going to read all the books and documents, files and notes that had accumulated since my visits to Rechnitz and Russia. I wanted to think, write, type a few sentences into my computer; I looked at the screen for hours, disliked everything I saw on it, got up to make coffee, picked up a book and, instead of reading it, looked at my reflection in the window. I watched myself standing in this strange apartment and acting as if I were reading, although I knew that I wasn't. Who did I think I was fooling?

*

'When I listen to what you're telling me today, it strikes me that you're short of male role models,' said Daniel Strassberg, my psychoanalyst. It was Wednesday again – or was it Friday? In the middle of the day other people went to the fitness studio. I'd spent that time, for months, lying on his couch. Those two hours belonged to my week now, had become part of my everyday life, and our experiment seemed to be working, because it hadn't been long before I'd answered my original question – what was left in me of the old days? – to my entire satisfaction. Of course Rechnitz, Aunt Margit, all that was still up in the air, but it was also far away until it stopped in front of my eyes, like a soap bubble floating along from somewhere or other – and burst.

'It's about what it means to be a man.'

'Is it?' I replied. I'd begun the session by telling him about my grandfather, my relationship to him, his years in the camp in Siberia, and the effect his time in Russia had had on my father.

'A family of weak men,' Strassberg went on.

I kept silent again. I felt annoyed, and my feelings were hurt. Who wants to hear a thing like that at mid-day on a Wednesday? Sunlight was falling through the little window, and I saw motes of dust dance in it. There was a small wooden figure with broad hips and thick lips standing on the bookcase; had he put it there by chance when he was furnishing his consulting room? Had he ever tried lying on his own couch to see what it felt like? Maybe, it occurred to me, he had slept here when it was late in the evening. Maybe he sometimes quarrelled with his wife and simply stayed here, smoking and reading and thinking. I was sure there was a bottle of cognac somewhere.

'In other words,' I heard him saying, 'the only person in your family whom you link with masculine attributes – power, money, sex, strength and violence – is your Aunt Margit, the monster.'

'Aunt Margit?' I said, startled. Her name hadn't been mentioned for a few weeks. I'd forgotten about her; other subjects had been more important, such as my work, my children. 'You mean a woman is my only male role model?' I was still looking at the wooden figure. 'And of all people . . . Margit?'

'Shit happens.'

I said nothing.

'Sorry,' he said, 'I didn't put that very elegantly. But do you see what I want to tell you?'

'No,' I said, although of course I did. I saw it all before me, myself, my father, my grandfather, my children. 'We went to the mountains at the weekend,' I started again after saying nothing for some time.

'Yes?'

'A family expedition. Other people do it all the time. But with us it all went wrong, and I lost control and hit my son.'

Strassberg did not reply.

'It simply happened. My hand slipped, as they say, and it really did. He looked at me with big, round eyes, like one of those cuddly toys, if you know what I mean, and I felt incredibly ashamed of myself. "You hurt me," he said, with his lower jaw quivering, and finally he began crying, I don't know anyone who cries so fervently, huge tears falling from his eyes; it always breaks my heart to see him like that. And what did I do? I tried to make light of it. "That wasn't anything," I told him. "I didn't hurt you." First I hit him on the upper arm, and then I deny it? I mean, isn't that pitiful?'

I waited to see if Strassberg would say anything, hoping for a word of encouragement, but there was no answer, so I went on.

'Then I picked my son up and said I was sorry. I went and told my wife about it. I felt like a puppy standing in front of her and hearing her say how useless I was, hitting my child and then saying I hadn't, and she was right. We were surrounded by those happy families with their happy children, and I got all worked up and couldn't take it any more. I couldn't stand myself, my reflection, my jokes, I wasn't comfortable in my skin, do you know what that feels like? When you can't say anything without listening to yourself. When you're always observing yourself from outside, like being in a fitness centre with mirrors on the walls where you watch yourself lifting dumb-bells in the air and you hate yourself for it. I was behaving badly, like when I was a teenager, and I didn't know what to do with myself all afternoon. Oh, what am I talking about?'

Strassberg still said nothing.

'When you were talking about weakness just now, that act of violence came into my mind. Why is it like that? I keep shouting at my children when I'm tired, or in a bad temper, and all they're doing is running around the apartment wanting to play. They want fun, they jump on the beds, but I hear myself telling them off, like a frus-trated pensioner. "Do you know how much that cost?" I shout at them when they break something, and I look angrily into their sweet little eyes, and then they giggle and run away. What kind of example am I setting them? I don't have anything to offer. That emptiness infuriates me, if you see what I mean. I remember one afternoon when I was about fourteen, and I went out with some friends, it was winter with snow lying outside. We took the bus to the swimming pool and began fighting as boys do at that age. We threw our caps down the aisle and slapped each other around the head with our swimming trunks. I was pushed off the seat, and suddenly I was lying between an elderly man's feet, and I realized he had my head caught fast – I remember that clearly, the smell of his boots, earth and leather, and the warm air of the heating in the bus. I struggled and pulled, but he kept his legs pressed together and wouldn't let me go. I didn't shout and call for help, instead I stayed calm, and he didn't say a word either – he just hurt me in silence. He was pressing as hard as he could; I felt his leg muscles quivering. Then I heard my friends shouting, 'Come on!' They had no idea of the fight I was engaged in. The bus stopped, and I managed to free myself by scratching his soft calves through his flannel trousers with my fingernails. I jumped out of the bus just before the doors closed again. My ears and certainly my face must have looked red. I'll never forget what his boots smelled like, I have that odour in my nostrils to this day. But why am I telling you all this?'

Strassberg still did not say anything, and nor did I. I looked up at the wooden figure, breathless as if I had been running. 'Damn it,' I said, 'am I like that man? Exerting quiet violence. What's become of me?'

Silence.

'A little Nazi in the nursery,' I answered myself.

14

One afternoon, when I was sitting at the desk in my friend's apartment, I picked up my grandmother's mud-green folder, the one that my father had given me after her death. It had been lying in a drawer for two years, unopened. I had found deciphering her handwriting too laborious. The first pages were about hunting and shooting, about pheasants and hares, subjects that really didn't interest me. But something else caught my attention: the voice in which she spoke was firm and strong, her resignation was gone, her fragility had disappeared. In writing about herself, her parents, and the events in wartime Hungary my grandmother sounded like someone who knew exactly what she was doing. Something seemed urgent to her, I understood that much.

The folder contained hundreds of pages, most of them handwritten, none leading on to the next in a consecutive narrative, which slowed me down at first, because I didn't know where to begin. Whole passages were crossed out; she had obviously revised them again and again, added comments, exclamation marks, and little asterisks referring to passages that I couldn't locate. Unlike a text written on a computer, where you don't see all the work behind it on its way to the final version, this was an open wound: her effort to find the right words, to achieve precision and truth, her despair, her anger, it was all clear on the page. She often wrote in the margin things that had occurred to her in reading her own words; these additions were unrevised, she wrote as fast as she thought, as one could tell from her flowing script. She was never satisfied.

I set out the pages on the floor, from the desk to the bathroom, from there to the kitchen, a long snake of white, unlined paper, and looked for the head of the snake, for some kind of order, for a beginning. If you are starting a jigsaw puzzle you look for the corners and edges first, but all that I kept finding was a name I had never heard before: Mandl. And the account of an afternoon in the inner courtyard of the family's castle in Sárosd in the summer of 1944, when the Germans marched into Hungary, Adolf Eichmann took up residence in the Astoria grand hotel in Budapest, and from there, within a few weeks, implemented Operation Margarethe: the occupation of Hungary, and the deportation of half a million Hungarian Jews to concentration camps.

*

'Did I tell you about my grandmother's diary?' I asked Strassberg. I was lying on his couch as I did every week, staring at the ceiling.

'No.'

'I've had it for a couple of years, but I didn't begin reading it until now. I thought it would be an old lady's harmless memoirs, but it seems to me that she was planning something larger.'

'Something larger?'

'A book. A confession. When she was dying, she told my father to burn everything, but he didn't. I'm the first person to read her diary.'

'What does she write about?'

'Her life. Her childhood. The time from 1920 to 1956 in Hungary. About growing up as the daughter of an owner of landed property, in a castle with an inner courtyard, with domestic staff, ladies' maids, a French tutor, a coachman. And then the war coming to that little village, Sárosd. The war changed everything. Hungary was Germany's ally . . .'

'I know.'

'The Jews were rounded up and sent to concentration camps,

or drowned in the cold waters of the Danube. The aristocracy were better off, but they too suffered. In the years after the war, all their land was confiscated and they were declared enemies of the people. She writes about that, about the change. She claims to have toyed with the thought of writing it all down for years, but she never knew how. Then, one morning, she woke up and saw it all in her mind's eye: the beginning of her book, the structure, the key scene. It was suddenly clear to her. It sounds like something in a film, but it's all there. The downfall of her world, my grandmother writes, began on an afternoon in the summer of 1944. She was obviously witness to a crime. A Jewish married couple died before her eyes in the inner courtyard of the castle.'

'When exactly did that happen?'

'I don't know. Their name was Mandl. They died in circumstances that aren't entirely clear to me. She says she could have saved them. *I can't look in the mirror without thinking of the Mandls*, she writes.'

'Mandl?'

'It's all confused. The sheets of paper are mixed up in no kind of order. It's like a crime story; may I say that?'

'Why not?'

'After all, two people did die.'

'Have you noticed that you're always asking whether or not you may do something? It runs right through your analysis; it's a search for legitimation: whether in your life, your career, your wishes and feelings, you always come up with that question. If you feel that this is like a crime story, then that's what it is to you.'

'No, I hadn't noticed. Why am I doing it?'

'We still have some work to do on that.'

Back in the apartment, I continued going from one sheet of paper to the next, found the beginning of one scene in the kitchen and its continuation at the end of the corridor. I began noticing the different pens my grandmother had used, and saw her in my mind's eye sitting up very straight at the table, a tall, thin woman with reddened nostrils. She will have been wearing a blue roll neck sweater, pale trousers, old-lady shoes with good soles. Jewellery? No, never. The reading lamp is on, the rest of the living room is in the darkness of late afternoon. It's likely that she has a glass of still water in front of her, with a pen beside it and maybe an apple on a white saucer. No, apples aren't in her line; walnuts are more like it. She takes out a paper tissue from the left sleeve of her sweater, tears a small piece off it, rolls it into a tiny pellet between her thumb and forefinger and puts it in her mouth. That's one of her few little quirks.

She's dissatisfied with everything but a few sentences. She crosses things out, corrects them, obliterates them, closes her eyes because the words won't come, because the sentences aren't right; *nem jó*, not good, nothing is the way she wants it to be. And when she opens her eyes again she sees groups of tourists in glaringly bright anoraks outside the double-glazed windows where condensation is collecting. Budapest is full of Chinese visitors in autumn.

She looks at the brown felt pen beside her glass of water. I imagine her picking it up, placing it at the top left-hand corner of the sheet of paper, and running it diagonally down to the very bottom of the page, until the dense brown colour fades. Then she writes, as a comment on the passage, after working on it for hours: *But these are all lies!* She has to press the pen down harder with every letter to get the last of the colour out of it.

I can hear the sound of the dry felt pen breaking the silence of her living-room, while the kitchen clock ticks in the background and the Chinese tourists in the square outside get back into their travel bus.

Nothing must be lost, she had always replied when I asked her why she spent hours on end writing, instead of simply sitting in the garden, or going for a walk. She also said something about an invisible band linking her world to mine. You just had to connect the separate parts and then you would see the link between grandparents and grandchildren, she said – it covered a hundred years, you couldn't survey more than that. Her parents were already too far away from me to be seen, my children too far away from her.

A hundred years? What link?

I didn't pay any attention to what she said when she was still alive. But the more I read her writing now, the closer I felt to my grandmother, as if she were trying to give me something to accompany me on my way through life. I studied her pages like a man possessed, deciphering passage after passage, like an archaeologist fitting tiny pieces of mosaic together in the hope of ending up with a picture. I spent days on the task.

It was the summer when men let their beards grow, women's T-shirts slipped off their shoulders, and thousands of people died in a civil war in Syria while I walked barefoot over my grandmother's history – and to a slight extent over mine as well. I still lay on Strassberg's couch twice a week and told him about my mosaic, in great excitement now. He was no longer the omniscient adviser that he had been in previous months, helping me to put things in order, but my ally. Our roles were less distinct, the hierarchy was breaking down. Going to his consulting room was like a visit to a café, Strassberg himself like a friend who always sat at the same table and had time to talk to me. And without thinking about it, I heard myself saying, 'I don't know if I could do a thing like that – hiding Jews.' I said it while the sun was shining over Zürich outside, the tram was going past, people were on their way to swim. I had already discussed so much with him, telling him the most intimate things about me, but only when I said that did I get a strange feeling as if I were hovering, as if I had reached a place where I had never been before. As if everything would suddenly make sense, although of course what I had said was absurd. Why would I have to hide Jews?

'That's your criterion,' he said.
'My what?'

'Your point of reference.'

'I don't understand.'

'The focal point of your life lies in the past.'

Was that, I asked myself in the bakery around the corner, deep in thought, the link that my grandmother had talked about? After every session with Strassberg I came here to buy a cheese sandwich and a Cola; it was always the same young woman behind the counter, with a baker's cap on her head, a ring in her nose, and a carp tattooed on her forearm. I imagined that I could see a line linking the generations with each other, still partly hidden in mist, but there was something there, a bridge over time. So many years, so many wars and borders lay between my grandmother and me, and yet what she said seemed to me familiar, as if we shared a secret.

'Will there be anything else?' the woman with the carp tattoo asked me.

'No, thank you.'

I could at least have saved the Mandls, my grandmother wrote again and again about that afternoon, describing the sound when the Mandls, husband and wife, fell to the gravel path in the inner courtyard, *but what did I do instead?* she asked herself. *Nothing.* She had done nothing all her life, had hidden and ducked aside, living like a mole – how did I come to know those remarks? Hadn't I said exactly those words a few weeks ago in Strassberg's consulting room, complaining of my lack of backbone, and how I hated my inclination to go underground? We suffered from much the same drawbacks, my grandmother and I – was that possible? Except that my struggles took place not in wartime but in offices and at the kitchen table.

'That'll be eight francs fifty.'

'What?'

'Eight francs fifty, please,' repeated the carp woman, stretching out her arm. The fish looked me straight in the eyes.

*

On the way to my friend's apartment, I persuaded myself that it was up to me to finish my grandmother's diary, filling in the gaps. I looked for anything about the Mandls on the Internet, and soon found the website of Yad Vashem, the memorial where the names and fates of all the Jewish victims of National Socialism are recorded, and I found the memorial page that Agnes had drawn up for her parents. It had been signed in Buenos Aires, with her married surname of Kupferminc. So Agnes must have survived Auschwitz, and had gone to Buenos Aires after the war. When I googled her surname, I found the home page of a woman painter, and I could tell, from her pictures, that I was at the right place. She must be the grand-daughter of the Mandls who had died in the courtyard of my grandmother's castle, there was no doubt of that.

*

A Wednesday again, and that couch in front of the white bookshelves. The head of the couch was level with the letter L. Lévi-Strauss, Lacan, Lukács, I knew all the spines of the books, and of course Leibniz, his works in one volume, from the Suhrkamp imprint, yellow lettering, *The Philosophy of Justice*. 'The Mandls had two children of my grand-mother's age, Agnes and Sándor,' I told Strassberg after simply lying there for the first few moments, rubbing my eyes and making sure that my sweater wasn't rucked up. 'They all played together as kids, I told you that, didn't I?'

'Yes, I remember.'

'My grandmother assumed that the Mandl children were gassed at Auschwitz. But they survived.'

'They did? How do you know?'

'Google. After the war, Agnes married a Pole who had also sur-vived the concentration camp. They had two daughters. I found one of those daughters on the Internet; she's a painter. She lives in Bue-nos Aires, and her name is Mirta Kupferminc. In her pictures, she studies the history of her parents and grandparents. I found an interview on her home page in which she says, ' One of the most important things in my life happened before I was born.' Isn't that crazy?'

Strassberg said nothing.

'She tells the journalist interviewing her that her grandparents took their own lives just before being deported to Auschwitz. They took poison to avoid the German gas chambers. But in her diary, my grandmother says they were shot. She was there, she saw it happen, she was an eyewitness and describes it in detail. Strange, don't you think? I also read, in an exhibition catalogue, that Mirta's creativity and desperation both derive from the trauma of her family's history. And in her works she would never destroy anything, only build it up. She finds old chairs by the roadside and fixes wings to them, she links Jewish traditions to modern life. She grew up, the catalogue says, full of nostalgia for the past, for history, old furniture, photographs, things that families hand down to each other from generation to generation, but she has nothing from the old days because after Auschwitz everything stopped. Whereas with me it's the other way round. I feel I have too much of what she doesn't have at all, do you see what I mean?'

'Yes, I do.'

'You were the one who told me my focal point lies in the past.'

'And obviously so does this woman Mirta's.'

'It seems to me that Mirta could just as well have been a nurse or a teacher, and then I'd never have found her. But no, she's an artist, and she doesn't paint landscapes or anything like that, she paints shadows of the past. I saw one of her installations illustrating the interview, *Skin of Memory*. She compares the number tattooed on Agnes in Auschwitz with the tattoos that young people get today.'

'What are you going to do now?'

'Write to her. Imagine, I could go and see her. And suppose her mother, suppose Agnes is still alive? What will I say to her then? I'm sorry about what happened? Let's forget it? My grandmother kept writing, like a kind of mantra: *I could at least have saved the Mandls. At least them.'*

*

Monday, 2 September 2013, 15:30
Subject: journalist from Switzerland

Dear Mirta Kupferminc
I am writing to you about something very personal. I have found a diary that belonged to my grandmother. Hundreds of pages. She was born in a little Hungarian village called Sárosd, in a castle. She says a good deal in this diary about your grandparents, the Mandls, husband and wife, and their children Agnes and Sándor. I'm assuming that Agnes is your mother, am I right?
There are some things that we really ought to discuss. They don't show my family in a good light.

Monday, 2 September 2013, 20:13
Re: journalist from Switzerland

Dear Sacha, what extraordinary news! I know your grandmother's name well, we've often talked about her, and I've been to see that castle in Sárosd myself. It really does look as if we have some things to discuss. Right now I'm at the airport in London, flying home in an hour's time. Maybe you could come and visit us some time? My mother Agi is nearly 90. I'm sure she'd be delighted.

Monday, 2 September 2013, 20:25
Re: journalist from Switzerland

Come to think of it, how did you find me?

Monday, 2 September 2013, 20:26
Re: journalist from Switzerland

I mean, how did you come upon the name Mandl? There are a thousand questions in my mind, I'm all confused.

Monday, 2 September 2013, 21:19
Re-re: journalist from Switzerland

Dear Mirta, finding you wasn't difficult. A few clicks, and I was on your home page where I saw your pictures. A thousand questions in your mind? And in mine too! I'd love to come to Buenos Aires and meet you and your mother. It says in the diary that my grandmother went looking for your mother in a Hungarian camp. But she didn't find her. Does that sound right?
You've been to Sárosd, that tiny village in Hungary. Guess where I'm going in a few days' time. We ought to talk on the phone.

Wednesday, 4 September 2013, 13:27
Re-re-re: journalist from Switzerland

Dear Sacha, I forwarded your email to my sister and other members of our family. They're all very excited. You'll understand, we don't get letters every day from people saying they know things about our grandparents. Do you have siblings yourself?

About your question: my mother was in Auschwitz, and before that in a Hungarian camp, so what it says in that diary could well be right. Only I have a question to ask in return: why did your grandmother go looking for my mother? I mean, what did she want from her? And what exactly will you be doing in Sárosd?

As you may know, we celebrate the Jewish New Year around this time, so I'm rather busy. But I'll be in my studio tomorrow afternoon. How about that?

Wednesday, 4 September 2013, 18:27
Re:re:re:re: journalist from Switzerland

Tomorrow will be fine. I didn't know about the Jewish New Year – I hope you have a lovely celebration! Do I have siblings? Yes, two brothers, one older than me and one younger. We can talk about everything else tomorrow, we have time now that we've 'found' each other.

Wednesday, 4 September 2013, 19:02
Re-re-re-re-re: journalist from Switzerland

Time? We don't want to lose any more of it. If I start crying down the phone tomorrow, don't let it bother you, just go on talking.

15

A few days later I boarded the train from Zürich to Budapest. It was cold and rainy, I sat by the window eating seedless grapes, with the folder containing my grandmother's notes on my knees. I planned to go on from Budapest to the village of Sárosd; I wanted to stand in the inner courtyard where the crime that was then kept secret for seventy years had been committed.

In contrast to all the other passages from the diary, it gives several different accounts of that afternoon. I had noticed that as soon as I opened my grandmother's folder and began laying out the sheets of paper on the floor. At first I thought there were revised, clean copies involved, only when I compared the versions with each other did I realize that they were getting increasingly detailed, longer, more graphic. As if my grandmother had needed to take a long run-up before approaching the heart of the matter. And instead of destroying the old versions, she kept them, perhaps as evidence of the long path she had taken in approaching the truth bit by bit. At the end of the first version, in which she didn't yet mention any shots, she wrote in brown felt pen: *But these are all lies!* At the end of the second, she asks herself: *But suppose it was much worse?*

There had been women in close-fitting sweaters standing on the platform in Zürich, wearing leather boots with pointed toes and stiletto heels, smoking a last cigarette before heaving their heavy cases into the train. I wasn't the only one to have noticed them, other passengers also looked straight at them and nodded surreptitiously, as if saying to one another: So those are the

Hungarian women that TV and the newspapers have been talking about for months.

One of the women was sitting beside me; she had a chihuahua in her handbag. It was licking the gold zip fastener as we went through the suburbs of Zürich. When she tried getting her case on the luggage rack, her sweater rode up, and her stomach emerged from her trousers and spilled over, like the milk I try heating for my children if I forget it on the hotplate. The gemstone in her navel was right in front of my nose. So we got into conversation.

If I could only manage to describe the events of that afternoon as they actually happened, I would be content, my grandmother wrote in her diary. *What did I see, and what am I imagining?* she asked herself. *Why was Mother in the sanatorium, and why am I giving all the members of my family an alibi? Why did I protect Father all his life, although he hardly took any notice of me? Isn't it time for me to expose him at last?*

'My name's Linda,' said the woman with the dog in a bored tone of voice, when I offered her some of my grapes and she declined them. 'Are you going home too?'

'Going home?' I repeated. 'Yes, in a way I am.'

I looked her way for a little longer, as if I were going to say something else, and she stared at her telephone as if waiting for a remark, but I couldn't think of anything else. It's easy for me to talk about the past in Hungarian, the language of my parents – or about food. I know the words for labour camp, land reform. My vocabulary contains many 19th-century words: Easter mass, horse-drawn coaches, apricot conserve, because I've heard them since I was a child. But when it comes to modern life, I am short of words. I don't know the Hungarian for headphones, trainers, jealousy, staggering, dancing, Twitter. The old-fashioned Hungary is the one I know, but here in a railway compartment with Linda and her chihuahua, just before midnight, that wasn't much use to me.

In Buchs, another Hungarian woman got on the train. She obviously knew Linda, because they immediately began talking to one another. They brought out biscuits, cola, chewing gum, and it went on all the time. If I closed my eyes, I hard the squeal of the carriages running over the rails, the rustle of a bag of potato crisps, and above all the sound of the garishly coloured plastic clips that both women had stuck to their fingernails, and that they kept moving over the displays of their mobiles. It was the characteristic sound of that night – like rats scurrying over linoleum.

Friday, 6 September2013, 23:15
Re:re:re:re:re:re: journalist from Switzerland

Dear Sacha

We're all kind of in shock here, since you and I spoke on the phone. The whole story is quite something, and it will be best if you come and visit us soon. We have a feeling that you know more about our identity than we do.

My mother has wondered, all her life, why her parents killed themselves. She didn't understand it. If it's true that, as you say, they died in some other way, that makes a difference to us. We have to think what to do now, whether to tell her, and if so in what way. I'd very much like to see your grandmother's handwriting. Will you bring the diary with you? Write and tell me when you're coming.

'What do you do in Zürich?' I asked Linda.

'I work in a restaurant, as a waitress.'

'Where?'

'A little place outside the city. You won't know it, no one does,' she said, looking as if she was about to yawn. And I wrote back:

Dear Mirta, am in the train to Hungary, can't reply now. I'll call you.

The train went into a tunnel. Once again, I couldn't think of any-thing to say to Linda. I've never been good at keeping a conversation going. My mind went to all the newspaper stories about Hungarian girls who looked like Linda, the pictures of prostitutes at the side of the road behind the railway station. A few months ago there had been an attempt to get them away from there to a designated zone in an industrial part of the city, a few open garages. It had been devised and set up by civil servants in collaboration with social workers, women's organizations and health experts. There must have been a number of meetings, round tables, concepts, file folders full of plans, lists and proposals for costing the scheme. People will have sat in offices with rubber plants standing in the corner, while they racked their brains: how do we get the idea off the ground? What's it to look like? Safety first, they will all have said, of course, the women's safety takes priority.

So why not red neon lighting on the back wall? Good idea! Application passed.

And what's it going to be called? Those garages, someone surely pointed out, need a name, if only for the media.

More meetings, new propositions went the rounds, someone applied his mind to some kind of wordplay on 'red light', but noth-ing came of it. Someone else wanted it in French, *amour*, *voiture*, that would sound more romantic.

'We ought to be objective about it,' the head of department will have warned them. 'You can never go wrong that way.' And they will all have nodded. Of course.

Soon after the scheme was launched, the television people

came along and showed pictures of the compartments in which transactions, as they put it, took place. The TV pictures showed pixellated men in pixellated cars into which pixellated ladies climbed. Red neon lighting on the back wall, then the camera moved up to show the evening sky above Zürich. And what happened after that? Did the man drive on, maybe go home, have something to eat – or go to the opera?

And what about the woman? Did she just go back to the starting point?

Saturday, 7 September, 00:19
Re:re:re:re:re:re:re: journalist from Switzerland

If you're in Budapest, go to the Holocaust Museum. There's a picture of mine in it. We can talk when you get back.
Mirta

The train stopped at Innsbruck, rain pattered on the window. I imagined Linda telling her parents at home that the restaurant where she works is very popular. She will give them small presents, maybe watches, anyone who's been to Switzerland brings watches home even if they're made in China. She'll say how expensive everything is, but the streets are clean. 'Just think, people go swimming in the lake. And there are swans whiter than the snow here at home,' she will say, but nothing about what it's like standing in front of those compartments every evening and getting into strangers' cars; what it feels like when the driver takes the ignition key out of his dark blue Mazda: the lights go out but the music stays on, volume setting three, not too loud, not too soft, nice and comfortable.

She tells him the price, thirty francs, she's learnt the numbers in German, there's nothing cheaper than a blow job on offer in

Switzerland. 'You can begin now,' he says in English, and 'Where are you from?' She wedges her chewing gum low down under her lip with her tongue, undoes first his belt, then the button of his black jeans. She pulls the zip, which doesn't work at first, but then he helps her. Together they get his trousers down to below his knees, his white thighs lie on the dark upholstery, Pharrell Williams is singing 'Happy'. Linda likes the song; she's seen everyone dancing to it all one summer. She sang it herself in the shower, 'Happy' with a deep A sound, almost an O. But now she bends her head, brushing the air freshener tree that hangs from the rear-view mirror and sways back and forth in the light of the red neon tubes.

'Because I'm happy . . .'

Her face is level with the radio, dark blue display, cursive script, Radio Top, 'the best songs of all times'. She breathes in the warm air coming from the engine and smelling of plastic, while she reaches into his underpants with her left hand.

'Because I'm happy . . .'

She takes his limp penis in her hand and presses it a bit, his sighs mingling with the music, 'Happy, happy, happy', and he puts his hand on the back of her head. She adjusts to his rhythm, ignoring the smell – she's good at that – takes his penis, which was lying on his left thigh like her chihuahua, in her mouth, while he makes himself comfortable in that position.

Linda won't be telling them that at home.

'I once worked as a waitress in Switzerland,' that's how her official story will run. Just as Herr Mandl and Frau Mandl officially committed suicide with rat poison from the stock of their delicatessen shop, that was the story told at the time, although they had been shot in the back, although they had fallen to the ground, and their pale grey raincoats had blood on them. *Who decides what's true and what is false? Who decides what history says?* my grandmother asks in her memoir.

The train went on. Salzburg lay behind us. I looked up. A few lights from isolated farmhouses could be seen outside. Who was still awake there? My face was reflected in the window, I looked tired, old, rings round my eyes, hair badly cut, beyond me the dark outlines of Linda and the dog on her lap. So who decides what's true and what is false? Who can turn a murder into suicide?

My grandmother wrote: *Whoever is in power.*

She had not been there when her father went to the local mayor that evening in 1944, and after that to the priest to tell them what they had to do about the incident. But that's how it must have been, she thinks at the end of her life. *He was still an important person at the time, the aristocracy were still in power, while a few years later we had no influence any more. The communists took not only our land but our strength away from us.*

It is perfectly possible that my grandmother's father had waited, all his life, for the truth to come out. Perhaps he even hoped for someone to tap him on the shoulder from behind and say: Tell me, what exactly happened back then? But no one ever did, and the story sank to the bottom of the marshes that surrounded Sárosd, from which my grandmother retrieved it years later and washed the mud off.

*

When I had told my father a week before that I was coming to see him, we had also discussed politics, we had talked about the Hungarian prime minister Viktor Orbán, much criticized all over the world, but my father idolizes him. The newspapers were full of stories about the 'little dictator', who had had a football stadium built next to his own residence. I had also read somewhere or other that a parliamentary member of the far-right nationalist Jobbik party had had the European Union flag removed and replaced by the old Hungarian flag of 1920, reminiscent of Hungary when it was a great power.

I was sure that my father had approved of that. He will have said, 'Oh yeah', in the accent of John Wayne in *Red River*, as he always does in such situations, and I mentioned it to him.

'Is that story about the flag true?'

'Oh yeah.'

'What's the point? Why that eternal mourning for past greatness?'

'You don't understand?'

'No. I mean, it's only a piece of fabric.'

'If you don't understand I'm sorry for you.'

'Why?'

'Because you don't know what it means to have a native land. If your native land is threatened, that's painful. And it's painful when it's taken away from you.'

'Painful? Native land? You sound like someone out of the Middle Ages.'

'When do you arrive, anyway? We can talk about it then.'

'I get in just before eleven in the morning, if I survive the night in this train. Will you come and meet me?'

'Of course.'

We came into Budapest at eleven-fifteen. It was a fine autumn day; I particularly liked Hungary in the autumn. I had come to take my father with me and see the castle where my grandmother lived before the war. And I wanted to see the hunting lodge they had moved into later, I wanted to walk through the woods and fields where she used to work when the country was already under communist rule. I helped Linda to get her case out of the train; she had put the little dog back in her handbag. We were at the end of the platform when I asked her if we could exchange phone numbers.

'What for?' she said, not uncivilly, more as if she were used to the request.

'In case you ever need my help. I speak German, I know my way around.'

'I don't need any help.'

'Fine, then.'

'Well, okay.' She dictated ten figures, a Swiss number. In the distance, my father was waving. He came towards us, but then stopped. Linda put her pink headphones on.

'Right, then,' she said.

'Right,' I said.

'Who was that?' asked my father, watching her disappear into the crowd in her high heels.

'Linda, a waitress from Zürich. She works in a restaurant outside the city, but you don't know it, no one does.'

We spent the next four days travelling in the past.

*

In Sárosd, we saw round the rooms in the castle, I picked up some of the gravel in the inner courtyard mentioned so often in the diary, and took photographs of the chestnut tree. The place where my grandmother had once lived with her parents, with Goga the lady's maid, with the saddlers, the gardener and the French tutor was now a care home for old people, social misfits and the marginalized. Carers walked around bringing the residents soup in grey plastic bowls. Where coaches once used to drive up, an old woman in a headscarf was pushing her walking frame along, and got stuck when its little wheels couldn't manage the gravel. We went on to the hunting lodge, and then to the *village at the back of beyond*, the last stage in my family's journey before they fled to the West. 'It must have been somewhere there,' said my father, pointing to a group of grey houses with small windows. 'Bloody Communism.' He had been cursing Communism for some time, and it reminded me of our trip to Moscow and his tirades against the Russians. 'Let's go and get something to eat,' he said.

'Vodka?' I asked, because I suddenly saw before me the scene when I had grabbed his collar, with my forehead right in front of his nose.

'I don't drink vodka with you unless I have a safety helmet on.'

After we had both ordered, I took the folder containing my grandmother's notes out of my bag and read aloud from them: *It's late in the afternoon. I am lying on the bed in my room, reading, with Tolstoy's* War and Peace *on my stomach. A shout tears me away from my daydreams.*

'What's that?' asked my father.

'Does the name Mandl mean anything to you?'

'No.'

I had asked someone else the same question weeks before. I had gone to Liechtenstein to visit my grandmother's sister; the two of them had spent their childhood at the castle together. After the war, Lilly had gone first to Italy, and she was now living in a little place near Vaduz.

'Herr and Frau Mandl, does that mean anything to you?' I asked her once we were sitting down. Lilly is 93 years old, and I had to repeat the question five times. 'M-A-N-D-L,' I shouted, until she looked at me as if I was crazy to be shouting in such a loud voice.

'Oh, they were the village Jews,' she said, putting her hand on mine. Once she would never have touched me, but the older the members of my family grow, the softer and kinder they become. I saw on her fingers the marks of the rings that she had worn all her life. I saw the fine skin on her fingertips, and imagined her doctor trying to take a blood sample and putting the needle in there, but not getting a single drop out. 'The Mandls had a little shop. I remember their bottled cherries very well – they were so sweet and juicy. I was in trouble if I got cherry stains on my dress. Did I ever tell you how strict our mother was? And as for our father!'

'Can you remember the summer of 1944?' I interrupted her.

'We had to have breakfast with him every morning, and we had to be freshly showered and in a good temper. He hated it if we were cross.'

'What happened that day?' I asked her.

'What?'

'The day when the Mandls died.'

'Would you like some more wine?'

'Yes, please.'

She stood up, groaning; she had been having backache for the last few months. 'You were there,' I repeated, sounding like a local radio station reporter. Only then did I realize how silly it sounded. 1944 was over seventy years ago, a whole lifetime. She shrugged her shoulders.

'Goodness, I can hardly remember yesterday,' she said, pouring wine into my glass. 'Why do you want to know that?'

'The Mandls were a middle-aged married couple,' I told my father in the restaurant. 'The village's Jews. They had a shop not far from the castle. In 1944, after the Germans occupied Hungary, they worked in the castle garden, along with a dozen other Jews. They asked us for help, it says here.' I tapped the folder. 'The Mandls wanted us to help them.'

'Us?' said my father, and he drank half of his beer.

'Us meaning our family,' I said. 'Your grandfather that you were so fond of.'

'Oh, so that's why you're here.'

'Yes.'

'Go on reading.'

The gravel in the courtyard is all churned up, I can see the deep tracks left by tyres. The Germans took over the ground-floor rooms a few weeks ago, every room in our house is full of soldiers, refugees, wounded men. The dogs are extremely agitated, Mother has been in a sanatorium for weeks. From my window I can see my father. He is standing on the drive with Herr Mandl opposite him, waving his arms. Frau Mandl shouts at him, they are wearing light-coloured raincoats too large for them. I see their Jewish stars, and I go downstairs, gravel crunches under my feet. Herr Mandl looks me in the eyes; my father does not turn round.

'Shall I go on?'

'Of course.'

'It gets to be uncomfortable reading.'

The waiter brought bread, salt, pepper and paprika.

'She wrote several versions of what happened that afternoon.'

'Why are you whispering?' asked my father.

'I wasn't.'

'You were.'

'Isn't it strange? Why did she never tell anyone how important that day was to her?'

'No idea.'

'Didn't you ever ask her what happened in the war?'

'Not often enough, obviously. Go on reading.'

'It was a secret she kept all her life. She wrote pages and pages about that one moment, but only a single line about the death of her second child, your brother. Why?'

'How would I know?'

'No one knows where she buried him. What did she do when the baby in her arms died? Did you never ask her?'

'Go on reading.'

'Why are you shouting?'

'I wasn't.' But I picked up the sheet of paper and looked for the place where I had stopped.

'They're on the way to a concentration camp, they'll die,' says Herr Mandl. He means Agi and Sándor, the Mandls' children. He says they are already on one of the trains. Frau Mandl is clutching her rake. 'Help us!' she shouts, 'help us, for God's sake, do something!'

'What trains?' asks my father. 'I don't know what you're talking about.' Frau Mandl screams, Herr Mandl goes over to him and takes hold of his collar, my father pushes him away. Herr Mandl falls on the ground and loses his hat.

'What are you doing?' my father shouts at him. Herr Mandl is sitting on the gravel; once a tall, corpulent man, now he suddenly looks small.

'My children are going to die. We're all going to die,' he replies, all red in the face, and he slowly stands up, takes his hat, knocks the dust off his trousers.

'Get back to work!' my father orders him, and at that Herr Mandl takes Frau Mandl's hand and says, 'I won't do anything of the kind. I'm leaving, that's all.' They move away, fast, stooping slightly as they run off, over to the pond.

'Stop!' shouts my father again, once, twice, until in the end he is bellowing, but the two of them don't turn back. I look at my father's face, I see his fury, his anger. 'Stop!' Then I hear the shots.

'Do you want me to read you the other versions as well?' I asked my father. 'They don't contradict each other, they just say what happened in more detail. And we don't come out of it well.'

'We?' he asks again.

'Well. In a kind of way, yes.'

'Who actually shot them?'

'A German. Wehrmacht soldiers were living in the castle at the time. Wounded men were put in the cellar and the outhouses. They were standing and sitting around everywhere, including on the bench under the chestnut tree. They'll have been smoking and talking. And one of them drew his pistol and fired. A fair-haired man, that's how she describes him, young, thin. Perhaps he's still alive, imagine that.'

'He could be.'

'He was never called to account for what he did, because officially it didn't happen. He killed a husband and wife and made a whole family now living in Argentina unhappy. That afternoon never lost its hold on your mother, whereas the soldier – oh, maybe he became a baker in Leipzig, or a geography teacher. Two children, small apartment, spent Saturdays in the stadium watching Lokomotive.'

'What?'

'Just an idea. Lokomotive Leipzig, the football club.'

'I see.'

'Let's say his name was Böhme, Klaus Böhme.'

'Böhme? Our neighbours in Zürich were called Böhme.'

'I know, but I can't think up another name at the moment. Let's say this Böhme was twenty years old in that summer of 1944, then he'd be – I'm just working it out – then he'd be of retirement age in 1989. Perhaps in winter, in the weeks when the Wall came down – a German life. Isn't that a crazy idea? I'm sitting here with you because of that Böhme.'

My father said nothing. The waiter brought our order. Game goulash.

*

Monday, 16 September 2013, 15:45
Re:re:re:re:re:re:re:re: journalist from Switzerland

Dear Mirta, I couldn't get in touch earlier, I was in Hungary, and my children take up my time at the weekend. I'm very sorry to hear how much that journal has affected you all. I hope that as well as the pain there's something in the way of reconciliation in it. Was it a mistake for me to get in touch? I could be with you in a month's time. Early in the morning on 14 October. It's a Monday. Would that be all right?

Monday, 16 September 2013, 22:20
Re:re:re:re:re:re:re:re: journalist from Switzerland

It wasn't a mistake. You're giving us answers to old questions that we've asked ourselves again and again. The 14th is fine. Would you like to stay with us? Shall I meet you at the airport? How was Hungary?

*

Daniel Strassberg asked me the same question when I had been lying on his couch for five minutes, not knowing what to say. I had a feeling that my narrative was boring him – always the same old stories. Hadn't I just heard him yawn?

'Hungary was very interesting,' I said abstractedly. 'My father reacted with surprising composure when I told him about the Mandls. He was strangely calm. Otherwise, not much happened.'

Strassberg did not say anything.

Nor did I.

'I get the feeling that your mind's not on this,' I said at last.

'What makes you think so?'

'You yawned.'

'Did I? I suppose that can sometimes happen.'

'Yes, of course.'

'Does it make you angry?'

'I'd understand it. I mean, I had to overcome my own inclinations to turn up here today.'

'You did?'

'I didn't know what to tell you. There's nothing new, I keep repeating myself. The air's gone out of it. The intensity I felt in the summer is over.'

'It's the end of the crime story.'

'What?'

'The crime story. You were saying, a few weeks ago, that it felt like a crime story.'

I paused. Then I said, 'Yes, that's right. The crime story. First Rechnitz, the diary, the Mandls, then Agnes, Mirta, all those stories flowing into each other. Yours, too.'

'You're right, these have been strange weeks for me as well. A time in which we were brothers.'

'Brothers?'

'To put it in plain psychological terms, yes. Brothers or sons, whichever you like. You with your story, I with mine. My father, who was working for a Zionist communist organization, smuggled Jews through Switzerland to Marseilles, where they boarded ships for Palestine, like Agnes's husband. And my mother, like Agnes herself, survived the concentration camps. My father was supposed to get her over the border – she was smuggled goods. But they fell in love, and I was the result. In my youth, and later as a student, I didn't want a Holocaust identity, I didn't want to be a son of the Holocaust, but it left its mark on me, and all that's come to the surface again in these weeks talking to you. Our two stories flowed into each other, as you rightly said. Do you know where the expression 'symbol' comes from?'

'No. Of course not. Whenever you ask me if I've read or if I know this, that or the other, I say no.'

'Why?'

'Because I feel stupid compared to you. But forget it. I shouldn't have said that.' I fell silent. What kind of idiot are you? I asked myself, and to get the conversation going again I said, 'So what about the word 'symbol', then? Where does it come from?'

'From Ancient Greek *sumbolon*, a mark or token. It was a means of recognition. A clay ring was broken in half, and one half given to the person leaving. Anyone carrying that half could turn up and stay with the other person, the one left behind. That's how our stories acted – they made up a whole. But I can see why you're complaining about the intensity going out of it. It's the same with love, and friendships, and in fact in psychoanalysis too.'

'Really?'

'I should tell you that when I was training I underwent analysis myself – everyone had to. One day I told my analyst I was sleeping poorly, and I concluded that I might have a problem with my girlfriend, and I couldn't allow anyone too get close to me. Guess what he told me?'

'No idea.'

'He asked how wide my bed was. I said one metre forty, and he advised me to buy a wider one, and that would solve the problem. I'd like to say that if I yawned it was just because I felt tired, there was nothing else behind it. Tell me about your journey. It really does interest me.'

'Just before I went to Hungary I phoned Mirta – you know, the painter, Agnes's daughter.'

'Yes, I know.'

'At the end of the conversation she said she felt as if she'd known me for a long time. And I felt the same. Not because our forebears had known each other back in the past, but because there was a curious sense of familiarity between us. Or perhaps I'm just imagining it. She told me how much her whole family felt linked to the story of her grandparents, and she was still trying to find out about it. How did I know all those things, she asked, so first I told her the harmless stuff, the description of the shop, the bottled cherries on the counter, and she shed tears of joy when I read out from the diary how her grandfather always had red patches on his cheeks. It seemed to me almost uncanny.'

'Uncanny in what way?'

'Her feeling so close to her grandparents, although they were people she'd never even known. The way every little detail moved her. At one point she asked me if there were passages in the diary that might shock her, and I said yes. I really wanted to wait until I'd deciphered all the pages myself, but she insisted, so I told her all I knew about the last fifteen minutes of her grandparents' lives. How they had worked at the castle, and had been helping in the garden with other Jewish families. How they asked my great-grandfather to help them, and then the quarrel, that scream, the gunshots. She began crying, and I didn't know whether or not to apologize.'

'Did you?'

'No, I kept quiet. She said she wasn't sure whether she ought to tell her mother about this new turn in the story. She was going to think it over and discuss it with her sister, she said.'

'Why is she hesitating?'

'It's too painful. Too much to expect of Agnes. Why torment an old woman who has suffered enough in her life with new information?'

'I don't understand that.'

'I don't understand it either.'

'Isn't it more painful to assume that your own parents killed themselves?'

Monday, 16 September 2013, 22:41
Re:re:re:re:re:re:re:re:re:re: journalist from Switzerland

Dear Mirta, no need to meet me, I'll take the bus into the city. I've found a hotel. Hungary was good, but I'm afraid I never made it to the Holocaust Museum. What does your picture there look like? Can we meet for lunch?

Monday, 16 September 2013, 23:03
Re:re:re:re:re:re:re:re:re:re: journalist from Switzerland

That would be nice. The Mott Restaurant, corner of El Salvador and Armenia. Is one p.m. all right?

16

But first, a flashback to Hungary in 1982. In the era of János Kádár, hated as he was, the country opened up. People felt a greater sense of freedom, wages rose, travel to the West was allowed, although it was very expensive. In those days many Hungarians indulged themselves with a few days of holiday near Lake Balaton, a hundred kilometres from Budapest, where more and more restaurants opened, and where there were campsites, small boarding houses, shoe shops for the women who walked along the roads in neon-bright dresses and liked it when men wolf-whistled at them. In the bathing resorts you could listen to Nena, Supertramp and Hungarian hits, you could eat deep-fried perch-pike, drink beer and genuine Cola as you looked out through the reeds at the water, and if you looked westward from Siófok over the water on a hazy day you could hardly see the opposite bank. It was as if you were at the seaside. On the Riviera, as this area was known, tourists also came from Bulgaria, travellers on package holidays from the Soviet Union, and above all families from the GDR. There were more beautiful places in Eastern Europe, to be sure, there were larger lakes in Poland, finer sand in Mecklenburg and better fish in Dubrovnik, but in Hungary everything seemed more relaxed and, at the same time, more progressive. 'That's how it is in the south,' married couples from Dresden told their daughters, who sat crammed together on the back seat of the family Trabant looking out of the windows, and marvelling at ice-cream parlours with mirror walls. From June to late August, a breath of freedom surrounded places like

Balatonfüred, where teenagers from Budapest tongue-kissed girls from Ljubljana or Leipzig in the evening outside the Disco Flört, smoked cigarettes with white filters, and drank schnapps punch, with chunks of water-melon soaked in the local plum brandy floating in it. Every evening the boys' favourite game was to take one of those girls down to the lake by night and out on the long landing stage, with its wooden slats still warm from the sun. There was a little boat tied up there, he jumped in, cleverly kept his balance, took her hand and helped her to sit in the bows, fitted the oars into the rowlocks, and steered straight into the reeds as usual. For her, however, it was all new: the bad smell of mud and silt, the stems of the reeds gliding by close to the planks of the boat, so that soon she could see nothing to right or left, only the dark sky above her.

Let's suppose that the girl now looking up at the sky and guessing what was about to happen bore the surname Böhme, and in these carefree summer days in the early eighties was camping with her parents and her sister in Siófok, in a brown tent with a canopy under which a folding table would just fit. During the day her father Klaus Böhme, aged 58, spent most of the time lying on his air mattress in the shade of the small pine wood that belonged to the campsite, with his portable radio to his ear. The football World Cup was going on in Spain, and he didn't want to miss any of the games, although the GDR was not involved, having lost the crucial qualifying match against Poland.

It was the second year running that the family had gone to Lake Balaton, to meet his wife's cousin and her husband from the West. Böhme's Trabi was parked beside the Mercedes belonging to his relations from Mannheim. Thousands of families usually separated by the Wall could spend a few days together bathing in Lake Balaton. Citizens of the Federal German Republic and the German Democratic Republic lay side by side on towels printed in colourful patterns, the former anointed with Hawaiian Tropic sun oil smelling of coconuts, the latter with Lebona walnut oil. You could tell from the design of the tents whether they came from the West or the East, but after a few days that made no difference. What hardly anyone knew was that there were also Stasi employees on the campsites around Lake Balaton, friendly, helpful men who said good day every morning, sometimes bought children an ice cream, and disappeared for a few hours in the afternoon into the hinterland, where they met their Hungarian colleagues and read out to one another what the subjects of discussion had been, and who disappeared with whom into whose tent.

When the family had arrived in Hungary a week before, Böhme had been well satisfied. The weather was good, he liked his wife's cousin although he thought her husband showed off too much – he had skimpier bathing trunks than anyone else, he wore the biggest watch, he was always giving his opinion on everything – but once Böhme had discovered the pine wood as a refuge he felt all right again, or would have done but for something that had been bothering him over the last two days, although what exactly was it?

Must be to do with my digestion, he told himself, that soured cream on all the food. He put on his shirt and beach sandals, picked up the leather wallet in which he kept his money and his sunglasses, crossed the campsite to the toilets, and from a distance saw his daughter in the middle of a group of young people. She was laughing, the sun had bleached her hair a shade blonder, and he hadn't failed to notice that she was coming back to their tent later and later in the evenings.

But instead of standing outside one of the blue toilet doors he simply walked on, past the restaurant, past the office where they had been shown the location for their tent, and suddenly he was beside his car. He didn't think much about it, or didn't want to think, he got in, started the engine, and wound down the window. It was hot, and the car smelled of the artificial leather of the seats as he drove over the railway lines and along the main road, the way that they had taken coming to the camp a week earlier.

His wife wouldn't miss him. Hungary was playing El Salvador early in the evening, but he could do without that. The wind felt good, his shirt fluttered, he would just explore the surroundings a bit, he thought, but of course Böhme knew where he was going.

To the east of Lake Balaton, the ground was hillier. He saw vineyards, overtook a blue tractor, and soon reached some marshes. He could tell that because there were hardly any trees in sight now, and no fields. After all, he was a geography teacher, and he also thought he could catch the smell of the marshes in the air. When Böhme reached Sárosd he slackened speed, drove past the gypsy huts on the way into the village, saw chickens and pigs and children sitting on the ground, drove on, passed low houses with reed-thatched roofs, saw storks nesting on chimneys, and the church tower. He stopped there, got out of the car, and realized that he was wearing only bathing trunks and a short-sleeved shirt, with his beach shoes. He couldn't walk about dressed like that, so he stood beside the car, rather undecided. He looked at the church, the shops selling food to right and left of it. Among the trees he saw the roof of the yellow castle that he knew so well. He wanted to take a closer look, just go for a little stroll, he told himself, and he crossed the road. Hadn't there been a stream somewhere near?

It was early evening, there was no one in sight. Böhme crossed a small bridge and found himself outside the park surrounding the castle. This was where the gravel path leading to the inner courtyard began. As he walked, he felt every pebble under his rubber soles. He wanted to see the inner courtyard, he'd only take a quick look at it, and there didn't seem to be anyone around, so he went the few metres along the castle wall, felt the heat coming off the masonry, saw the branches of the chestnut tree, and then he remembered its mighty trunk. Wasn't there a circular bench round it? He'd soon see it, another few steps, and when he turned the corner and was suddenly in the courtyard he saw the tree. He had spent whole afternoons in its shade during the war. But now there were no soldiers sitting there, only a dozen elderly men and women with hospital gowns covering their bony bodies. Some were carrying medical infusion bottles, and they all stared at him, Böhme, in his bathing trunks and beach sandals. Just under forty years ago people had stared at him in this very place, but he was wearing uniform at the time, and carried a gun.

Back in the car, he struck the steering wheel with his hand every time an image from the past flashed before his eyes: the traces of powder from his gun, the sound of that couple collapsing on the gravel. How long ago, he wondered, had that been? He left the marshes behind, the first vineyards were coming into sight; did all that really happen, or was he only imagining it? Böhme drove back to the lake, soon he saw the first shops with air mattresses and water melons for sale. He heard children shouting – that reassured him. He let a family cross the road, and when they moved away, giving him a clear view, he saw a restaurant on the bank of the lake and steered his Trabi to its large car park. It was just after nine.

As there was no vacant table, he sat down beside an elderly gentleman, ordered a Soproni, and heard men clapping and shouting jubilantly in the background. Böhme got up and went over to the TV set. Hungary were leading two-nil against El Salvador. When his beer came he gulped it down. Only now did it occur to him that he had had nothing to eat or drink all afternoon. The men shouted again; Böhme instinctively looked at the TV and saw the repeat showing of Hungary's third goal. He came back to the table and ordered another beer. 'Football,' he said to the elderly gentleman, who nodded.

The inner courtyard, that gravel, the gunshots – at the latest by the time the score was four-nil and Böhme was on his third glass, he had successfully suppressed all that, sending it back to where all uncomfortable thoughts end up. Only the reddish earth on his beach sandals showed where he had been.

Let's suppose that the other man at Böhme's table was Russian, short hair, round paunch, and let's say his name is Andrei Simanovsky, civil servant, married, no children. 37 years before he had been a guard in a prison camp in a small town called Asbest. In 1955, under Khrushchev, when the last prisoners of war, including my grandfather, had been sent home, he began working for the railways and liked it. He travelled round the country a good deal, never stayed longer than a few months anywhere, and on his journeys he often thought back to his time as a prison guard, remembering not so much the prisoners, whose faces he had almost forgotten, as the atmosphere among the camp supervisors, all that drinking, the constant orders that he had to carry out, his fear of doing something wrong. When he least expected, in Lubansk on one of his journeys of inspection, he met his wife Julia, with whom he was now spending the summer holiday beside Lake Balaton. Every year a group of Soviet railway officials and their wives were allowed to go on holiday to Hungary, and this year it was the Simanovskis' turn; ten days on the Riviera, what a piece of luck! Simanovsky was a good husband; he drank, but never very much; he was conscientious, loyal, a quiet man who never felt at ease in large groups, and was still happy to be on his own for a few hours. Even as a child he had liked to be alone, but now, sitting beside this German in bathing trunks who drank beer as if it were water, he felt, to his surprise, how much he missed his wife.

BÖHME   In 1982, he is 58 years old, married, the father of two children; he is tall
and thin. He is a teacher of geography and chemistry at a school in Leipzig.

SIMANOVSKY   Five years older than Böhme, also married, has a son by a
brief affair but never sees him. Instead, he has a dog. A lover of classical music,
he is particularly fond of the second movement of Tchaikovsky's piano trio in
A minor, op. 50, and also of the closing movement of the Symphonie
Pathétique.

TIME   June 1982. In the Falklands War, Argentina has surrendered. NATO sum-
mit conference in Bonn, 350,000 people demonstrate against Ronald Reagan's
plans for nuclear armaments. Paul McCartney and Stevie Wonder take
over from singer Nicole's 'Ein bisschen Frieden' [A Little Bit of Peace] at the
top of the German charts, and Steven Spielberg's *E. T.* breaks all records at
cinemas.

PLACE   The Good Perch-Pike restaurant, Balatonvilágos

Of course this is unlikely. How would these two particular characters meet? But if
you stop to think how many Germans and Russians of that age had led similar lives,
and as soldiers, informers or guards had contributed to the two totalitarian systems
that marked Europe in the last century, perhaps without being aware of it, then those
two gentlemen in their short-sleeved shirts were average people with average life
histories, now in the last one-third of their average lives, and were haunted on some

days by their average past, a phenomenon manifesting itself in the form of mild melancholy and fits of bad temper, wearing off as suddenly as they come. Böhme and Simanovsky were human beings like ourselves.

BÖHME   You're Russian, aren't you?

SIMANOVSKY   Yes.

BÖHME   I studied Russian at university. That's thirty years ago now.

SIMANOVSKY   You speak it well.

BÖHME   Oh, well. Don't you like football?

SIMANOVSKY   No, it never interested me. How about you?

BÖHME   I take a bit of interest in it, yes. (*Neither says anything for a while.*)

SIMANOVSKY   What else did you study?

BÖHME   After the war I studied chemistry in Leipzig. They were saying at the time in the GDR that our young country would need new teachers, so I registered for that. Then the Wall was built, as you'll know. Now I teach chemistry and geography. I like teaching, I enjoy it. Most of the time, anyway. I'm sure you know how it is. Do you have children?

SIMANOVSKY   No. Well, yes. It's a long story.

BÖHME   Are you ...

SIMANOVSKY   I'm married, my wife has gone bowling, but I had a headache so I didn't go with her. How about you?

BÖHME We're camping in a tent near here. My wife and my two children. I've
  just been, well, I went for a little drive, I . . .

Shouts of jubilation in the background. Böhme looks in the direction of the TV set,
but he can't see anything; men in swimming trunks, smoking, hide his view of the
screen. 'Who's playing?' asks Simanovsky. 'Hungary,' says Böhme, standing up with
his beer glass in his hand. He takes a couple of steps forward, cranes his neck and
watches the repeat of the goal, five-one in the 64th minute. He'd like to be watching
the match now, but it's too late for that.

SIMANOVSKY Where did you go?

BÖHME What?

SIMANOVSKY You were saying you'd been for a drive?

BÖHME Yes, you see, back then I was stationed near here. Long ago. A lot has
  happened since then.

SIMANOVSKY Yes, I understand.

BÖHME But I can't complain, we're doing all right, don't you think? Hungary,
  a summer holiday, I mean . . . I could do with another beer. How about you?

SIMANOVSKY (nods)

BÖHME I just drove around for a while, looked at the countryside – the
  marshes, the villages, so many nice people, know what I mean?

SIMANOVSKY Absolutely.

Another goal; it's seven-one to Hungary.

BÖHME   Cheers.

SIMANOVSKY   Cheers.

BÖHME   Did you study yourself?

SIMANOVSKY   No, I wanted to, but it didn't work out. I was in the army, you know how it is. You can't pick and choose. I work for the railway administration now.

Eight-one to Hungary. The other men are cheerful, remains of beer foam dry on their moustaches, the air is sultry, the sun set long ago. The game goes on for another twenty minutes. Böhme and Simanovsky sit in front of their glasses, looking at the table; they don't know what else to talk about, they are tired and slightly drunk, not in the pleasant way but in the other, melancholy, crippling manner. Böhme stares at his beer glass; he doesn't want to go back to the tent just yet. Simanovsky thinks of the travel group. Maybe it's about time he was getting back? He thinks of his dog at home, wishes the dog was here with him now. More jubilation, the score is nine-one; Böhme doesn't react any more, he gets a feeling that he can't move his arms and legs, while the voice of the Hungarian commentator cracks with excitement. The game goes on another ten minutes. And when Simanovsky finally signs to the waitress, Böhme is relieved and feels that he would like to say something to the Russian stranger, but as he can't think of anything, and is ashamed of that, he takes the bill. 'No, no,' says Simanovsky, protesting, but Böhme won't retreat from his offer although it suddenly seems to him excessive. However, he can't do it.

BÖHME   I enjoyed our little talk.

SIMANOVSKY   Me too.

They shake hands for a little longer than is usual, the score is ten-one to Hungary, the referee blows the whistle, the game is over, El Salvador is put out of its misery, and so are the two men.

17

I entered the Mott Restaurant in Buenos Aires just before one o'clock. It was a large room, flooded with light, and had once been a garage. The restaurant tables were dark wood. Mirta stood up and waved; I recognized her from the photos on her website, her glasses with their colourful frames, her smile. I had read all the Google entries about her, had clicked on her installations. We had become friends on Facebook before we met for the first time. Now I crossed the room, and was wondering how to greet her when she put out both hands, as people do when they meet again after a long time. A little later her sister Marga arrived. She was more restrained than Mirta, spoke more softly, choosing her words with care, and so the three of us sat at that table in the middle of South America and began at the beginning again, as if the emails and phone conversations had never taken place.

'I usually eat salmon here, but I'll have the tuna today,' said Mirta. 'A steak for you?' she asked me.

I nodded.

'Rare?'

'Yes, please.'

I showed them photos of my children in swimming trunks, with water wings, on the banks of a Swiss lake, ketchup at the corners of their mouths, and they brought out their own phones and showed me family photographs. 'Our whole family feels connected with Hungarian history,' they said, while I looked at all the strange faces with eyes showing red in the camera flash. 'Whenever any of us has gone to Europe in all these years, we've tried to find out more about ourselves.'

'But why?' I asked. 'Does it never end? Isn't it odd that even your children are still wrestling with the past?'

'So are you, aren't you?'

'Yes, you're right. Although I always wonder if that's the best thing to do, or if one shouldn't let sleeping dogs lie.'

'What for?' they asked, not in a mocking tone, but I could hear that they had often considered that question before; there was something routine in the response. 'We grew up,' said Mirta, 'with the idea that our lives today are determined by the painful past. It's our inheritance. It's always been there, in every minute of our childhood, every hour of our youth, every day of our lives.'

I nodded, and found my thoughts drawn to the lake that I had just shown them in the photos, the pebbles on the shore that you had to cross to reach the water. I often took my children swimming, and spread brightly coloured towels out for them in the shade of the trees. Sometimes there was pollen on the meadow. Later I would buy them a sausage, an ice cream, just as my parents used to do when my brothers and I were little. Was that enough for us to say we had put down roots in Switzerland? Was it something I wanted to hand on to my own children, or was it too ordinary? The contentment when you set off for home, tired after bathing, the sun in your hair, the smell of wet swimming trunks in a plastic bag. Mirta and Marga had the Holocaust to cling to – what did I have?

We drank to each other. I told the sisters about time, about Rechnitz, and how I had come by my grandmother's diary. They told me about their father Aron, who had been married before he met Agnes and had lost his wife and their baby in Auschwitz. 'Unlike our mother Agi, once the two of them came to Argentina on that ship in 1948, Aron never wanted to hear about Poland again.' They had grown up in poverty, said the two sisters, they hadn't even had a bathroom, but everything had been neat and clean – 'very

European,' they added. Only two things were left from their parents' earlier lives, they told me: one was the photograph that Agnes had sewn into a margarine box in Auschwitz and had smuggled out past the guards. 'It's behind glass in a frame at my place these days,' said Mirta. The other was the belt that Aron had made a German soldier give him on the day of his liberation from Auschwitz. Now that the war was over and he had escaped the gas chambers, he didn't want his trousers falling to his knees the whole time. It was a question of dignity.

'Mirta has the photo, and I have the belt. It hangs on my wall,' said Marga.

'His belt?'

'Yes.'

'Of course,' I said quietly, as if nothing could be more normal than to have an Auschwitz guard's belt hanging from a nail on your wall.

'We flew to Hungary with Agi ten years ago to look for our grandparents' grave,' said Mirta. They had received some new information, telling them that in the spring of 1944 all the Jews of the area around Sárosd, including their grandparents, were made to leave their homes. They had been herded together like cattle and accommodated in farm buildings in the neighbouring village.

'Then the Germans must have sent them from there to my grandmother's family and the home farm of the castle, that's what it says in the diary,' I interrupted the sisters, looking through it for the place. 'Just a moment, here it is.' *From that day on*, I said, reading aloud, *about twenty Jews came to the farm every morning. They wore yellow stars on their jackets. The Goldner brothers helped with the horses, the Medaks and the Mandls worked in the garden, the rest went out to the fields.*

'They cleared out the stables,' I said, 'they pulled out weeds and cleaned the carp ponds.'

'They were your slaves,' said Mirta.

'Ours?'

'Your family's.'

I read on. *We knew many of them, we wished them good day, and they greeted us back. But those who didn't know us were too frightened to look us in the eyes – what had we done?*

On that journey to Hungary, the sisters said, they had found a name and the cause of death in an archive: Mandl, suicide. 'There it was in black and white, and for the first time we had an official document proving that our grandparents had existed – and saying how they died,' said Marga, looking at me wide-eyed. 'Do you understand how important that moment was for us? For the first time they weren't ghosts any more, they were real.' And I nodded, but I was lying. I couldn't really understand it.

They had been all churned up that day, said the sisters. On the outskirts of the cemetery, beyond the bushes, where everything was overgrown with plants, Agnes had found a weathered stone without any inscription, and they had decided to say that was their grandparents' gravestone. My steak had arrived on the table now; I cut it up, sawing through the fat and the meat fibres, the red juices collected at the side of the plate and ran into the potato salad. 'We suddenly felt sure that we were very close to them.'

'Suicide?' I asked.

'Yes.'

'Then why does it say something else in the diary?' I pointed to the folder, which I had on my knees covered by the fabric napkin.

'That's what we wonder, too.'

We went on eating in silence.

'Who committed the crime?' they asked after a while. 'Your family? Who hushed it up?'

'A German soldier from the Wehrmacht shot them – a tall, thin man, that's all my grandmother says about him. But she writes that her father hushed it up. It was easy for him. He was powerful, he had influence, he made up the story you were told, or that's how we'd put it today. A single phone call would have been enough for some official to write down in the records what you found in the archives. It must have happened something like that; I'm sure that's the most likely version. There were telephones at the time, weren't there?'

We arranged to meet again that evening. Mirta asked me to bring my grandmother's diary, and could I get the pages photocopied? I spent that afternoon in the rain, which had been falling for days, there were floods in Paraguay, I saw photographs on TV, a bus had tipped over and was filling up with pale brown water. I was going to sit in a café, but couldn't decide which; one was too noisy, another too expensive or too full, so I went on walking, and when I saw my reflection in display windows, my untidy hair, the white patches on my wet scalp, those ridiculous shoes with coloured soles that are usually worn by teenagers, I felt like screaming. Go on, I told myself, why don't you scream? I've known such thoughts since my youth. Why do you never see people in the street who suddenly stop and scream? Or collapse and can't go on? Where do we all get the strength to control ourselves? When my eldest daughter was born, and I found out for the first time how she screamed and raged, as babies do, I was concerned, like all new parents, and after a while it got on my nerves, but most of all I was surprised. Wasn't she doing what I wanted to do myself, only I kept my screams quiet?

That evening I sat at the supper table with Mirta and Marga and their husbands. We talked about all sorts of things: Hungary, Switzerland, the rain. And when we had finished eating I took out the notes and began to read them out, first in German, then in English, searching my head for the right translations: *chestnut tree, pebble, sour cherry*?

I hadn't thought about it before, but only now did I notice how important every single word was, because it laid a trail to which they would refer back. What I was saying belonged to these people, and yet I was the one deciding on their past. I chose the words, and now I was writing the story, now I was the one who had power – what kind of a feeling was that?

Someone had put a glass of whisky on the table in front of me, and I looked at the ice cube coming to the surface while I read the passage about their grandparents' shop, the well-stocked shelves, the scales on which Herr Mandl weighed out sugar, flour, apples in autumn – adding a little extra at the end.

'How nice to hear that he was generous,' said Marga, and her eyes, where the tears had dried, were shining.

I read about the train with its roof sparkling in the sun that my grandmother had seen one Sunday from the fields. *The Jews are in there*, someone had whispered, and she hadn't been able to take her eyes off the train until it moved away again.

I read out the passage in which my grandmother went to look for Agnes in a Hungarian prison before she was deported to Auschwitz. The two girls had almost met, it said in the diary, but it didn't actually happen. Then came the different versions of the afternoon when the Mandls died. I began with the shortest one, then the second, then the third. All of them round the table were hanging on my lips, I could feel that, as they heard the words and made images from them. *Herr Mandl took his wife's hand*, I read, *he crossed the courtyard. 'Stay where you are!'* someone called after him, but he had no intention of obeying, he went on to the pond and was going to cross the bridge, perhaps going back to his shop, when the soldier drew his gun. Mirta and Marga had handkerchiefs in front of their eyes. 'A brave man,' they said, through their sobs. 'Like us, he wasn't going to be ordered about.' I sipped my whisky, felt the pleasant sting of it in my mouth, the warm sensation first in my ribcage and then in my stomach. After a silence that lasted for some time, they asked me why I had really come to Argentina.

'Why?'

I was rather surprised. As I had been some years earlier, when the writer Maxim Biller had asked me, in company, what I felt I my great-aunt Margit was to do with me. Margit, who shared some of the guilt for the massacre of 180 Jews in Rechnitz, and me? Nothing,

I had said, but my embarrassment had told me that was not the whole story, just as I realized here how little weight my answer now carried. 'I'm only the messenger,' I said, the bringer of news, but that was not quite right. For when they asked me again whether I could let them have the pages of the diary concerned with what had happened to their family, I nodded and said, 'Of course,' but in fact I wasn't too happy about that – the story was also the story of my own family.

'The Mandls died in your courtyard,' said Mirta's husband. 'If I get the drift of it correctly, your grandmother could have helped them, but she didn't?'

'Yes,' I said. They died in our courtyard? My courtyard? Was I more than the messenger after all? 'She suffered for it all her life,' I quickly added, and it sounded like an apology.

'She went to look for Agi in a prison?'

'She went to the town of Kistarcsa and asked a soldier there if she could speak to Agnes Mandl. To be honest, I have asked myself, too, whether she really went there, or only wished she had gone. Because to go away from Sárosd she'd have had to leave her child behind with her parents, and in addition she was pregnant again, the country was full of Germans, the situation wasn't at all clear.'

'She was there,' said Marga into the silence, and because she felt cold she rubbed her arms. 'A few years ago I was sitting in the living-room with our mother, the same as every week, when she suddenly began talking about her time in the prison between camps. Someone had come looking for her there, she said, someone wanted to talk to her. 'Who was it?' I asked, but she didn't know. She had been so frightened then, she was still young, all on her own, without her parents, without her brother. But now at last we know who that someone was. It was that brave woman your grandmother.'

We all looked at one another as if we had solved some kind of puzzle.

173

'And suppose they had met?' the others asked me. 'What would your grandmother have said? I'm sorry your parents had to die in our courtyard?'

'I don't know,' I replied, and before I could say any more someone rang the front door bell, a shrill sound that startled everyone at the table. Mirta and her husband frowned; who could it be? They weren't expecting anyone, at this time of night, and today of all days. Mirta stood up, opened the lock, pulled the chain aside, and we could hear her greeting several people. Then her eldest son, his girlfriend and her parents came in, and he announced that he and the girlfriend were getting married next year, whereupon everyone first looked at each other and then stood up, their thoughts still with Agnes in the camp, and hugged one another. Mirta was weeping with joy when she took her son in her arms, her mascara already smudged from the tears that she had shed earlier.

*

Friday, 15 October 2013, 09:45
Re:re:re:re:re:re:re:re:re:re:re: journalist from Switzerland

---

Dear Sacha

You can imagine how much I had to think about last night. My son's arrival and the happy news of his engagement confused everything. So as for what we were talking about just before he rang the bell, just now I have to let rest for a while. Our story is being rewritten, and that's an enormous thing for us. I was thinking recently that it means, for instance, all the Google entries about me saying something about my past were wrong. Things that I said years ago aren't right any longer. That may seem to you a minor detail, and so it is, but it shows the extent of all this.

When we said goodnight, you said how surprised you were to find yourself so shaken by all this. I guess you're beginning to sense how much things that happened before we were born can affect us. Right to our innermost fibres. It keeps happening to Marga and me all the time. That's the inheritance we spoke about. Don't be afraid of it.

Thank you very much for coming to bring us this story – a story that belongs to us, and a little bit to you, too, because you decided to tell it. We'll see you at my mother's place. Shall we pick you up?

Friday, 15 October 2013, 11:53
Re:re:re:re:re:re:re:re:re:re:re:re: journalist from Switzerland

---

Dear Mirta

No need to pick me up, it's not far from the hotel – and by then surely it should have stopped raining, don't you think?

18

The first I saw of their mother was the walking frame that she was pushing ahead of her. Agnes came out of her bedroom. She had put on make-up, done her hair and prettified herself for me. Mirta and Marga, standing there with her, were pleased to see their mother like that. 'This is your visitor from Europe,' they told her. 'The grandson.'

'Who?' she asked, in slightly too loud a voice.

'You know, the grandson.' But Agnes didn't know; I could see that from her face.

We greeted one another, and sat down at her circular living-room table. I was just passing through, that was how her family had prepared Agnes for my visit, telling her that I had found information about her in my grandmother's diary. 'About your parents,' they said, about a time seventy years ago. And now, they told her, I was here to read her a few extracts from it.

'How wonderful,' she said, and looked at me. She hesitated, and then went on, in her thin voice, 'Are you Maritta's grandson or Lilly's?'

Now it was coming back to her.

'I'm Maritta's grandson.'

'Is she still alive?'

'No, but her sister Lilly is.'

'What?'

We were sitting side by side, almost touching. I could see the number tattooed on her arm in Auschwitz. It was disappearing into the folds of her wrinkled skin now, leaving the figures barely legible. 802 . . . 6? Or was that an 8? 'Lilly is still alive,' I told her.

'Oh, that's nice.'

Agnes spoke Hungarian, Spanish and German, sometimes changing languages in mid-sentence as she told me about my grandmother, who had been tall and slim and dark-haired. As children, they used to see each other every day, although they never talked much. 'You couldn't simply talk to everyone in those days,' she said, and I remembered that on the previous evening some one had told me about the German nanny who had looked after Agnes and taught her to speak German. 'It saved her life in the concentration camp. A German nanny, think of that.'

There were two flavours of strudel. Agnes told me how well her father got on with my family. 'They were special people,' she said. 'Good neighbours.' So far as the rest of us in the room were concerned, that took our breath away.

Good neighbours?

On the previous evening I had agreed with her daughters to keep the truth to myself. She was too old, they thought, too frail, she had heart trouble, she wouldn't be able to cope with it, so I went along with them and put on a show for Agnes. It was a very strange feeling, all of us in league, preserving our silence so that nothing would trouble her. Agnes had seen Auschwitz, the ovens, she had faced Mengele on the ramp – that's enough for one human life. Why, at the age of nearly ninety, should she be given the news that her mother and father had been shot in the back?

'Your dear family looked after our plants in winter,' Agnes went on, and her daughter seemed surprised, because they had never heard that before. 'There was a little hothouse next to the castle,' she remembered, 'and they let us put our flowering plants there so that they wouldn't die.' They had been so helpful, Agnes said, looking at me. 'There were others in the village who called me a "stinking

Jewess".' She said the first word in German, the second in Spanish, both coloured by her Hungarian accent, *stinkändä judía*, while she used her thumb to help her slide a piece of strudel on to her fork. Her father had even had their surname of Mandl changed to Merő because it sounded more Hungarian. 'He thought that would be some use against the Nazis and the Germans would spare us, but it didn't help.' 'The smell of Jews', she remembered, had been one of those terms that she often heard at the time. 'But not from the people in the castle, they were different,' she said, turning back to her plate as I thought of my grandmother's parents. So you took in the Mandls' plants in winter to keep them from freezing? Fresh earth and a nice place among the roses and begonias? How kind of you.

And what about the human beings?

They pleaded with you, I thought. 'Help us!' Their children were already on the trains, but you acted as if you didn't understand them. Why didn't you do anything? You could have hidden them – didn't the whole damn land around the castle belong to you? The forests, the stables, a single word from you, and the priest would have helped too, the farmer, the coachman. Why didn't you say that word? Was the risk too high? Or were you too concerned with yourselves, with the slow downfall of your entire class, were you too lethargic, indifferent and tired, as my grandmother says in her diary: *Mother was in the sanatorium, always in a bad temper, always ill. Father liked to go hunting best.*

And it wasn't just the Mandls you could have helped, I thought, as Mirta put another slice of strudel on my plate. What about all the others who toiled away for you daily at the castle? The Medaks? The Goldners? What about them? All gone to the gas chambers?

Did you never ask yourselves what became of them? Did they haunt you in your sleep? Did you hear their cries? And later, after the war, when the communists took everything away from you and you had to live in a little farmhouse, no coachmen, no ladies' maids, no status and power, were they with you then in that little kitchen, their weight heavy on your shoulders?

And did they also weigh down on my grandfather's shoulders later, on my father's, and now on mine?

No, that would be too simple. Or would it?

'Did you know Goga the lady's maid, Mami?' one of her daughters asked Agnes. It was strange to hear that name in a living-room in Argentina – Goga, whom I had read about in the diary: *Goga looked the way children paint the sun*. I liked that description. My grandmother must have loved her, perhaps more than she loved her mother.

'Who?'

'Goga.'

'No,' replied Agnes, while I wondered whether there might also be surviving descendants of the others who had worked at the castle: grandchildren of the Medaks, children of the Goldners, what had happened to them? For the fraction of a second, I saw images of those parallel lives in my mind's eye, maybe somewhere in America? They would be drinking weak coffee from large cups, going to their air-conditioned offices and celebrating Thanksgiving. How many people are there in the world whose lives might be different if my grandmother's parents had helped them? I was sitting in the living-room of one of them at the at moment, but how about the others? A network of people distributed all over the world. And if you visited them all, would you find some common bond between them? Wasn't I one of them too – and the thought alarmed me: wouldn't I myself have been different if they had done something at the time, instead of simply standing by and watching?

'You know,' said Agnes, 'a great many people in the district knew us; we were the Jews who kept the shop. But I knew hardly anyone. We scarcely played at all with the village children in the street, and only seldom with those in the castle.' The aristocrats, she said, hadn't had an easy time after the war. 'They had to suffer too, not in the same way as us, of course, but everything was taken from them. I have only good memories of that family.' Once again we were silent, shame-faced as we looked at our plates. But it was all the more of a relief to see Agnes happy. We were lying in a good cause, that was our pact.

I picked up the diary. That morning in my hotel I had marked the passages I was going to read aloud. I did not make anything up, but I left out a good deal that might have clouded her image of the old days. *The shop kept by the Mandls was magical,* I began. *Small and dimly lit, but in the twilight everything began to sparkle.*

'What?'

Began to sparkle, I repeated in a louder voice. *There were bags of sugar on the shelves behind the counter, figs, onions, and sausages hung from the ceiling, and there were sacks full of walnuts and apples standing in the corner.*

'Apples, yes, I remember that.'

Large glass containers stood on a yellow table beside the till, with brightly coloured sweets and sour cherries preserved in syrup inside them; there was a sweetish smell in the air, and a slight smell of petrol too, because the Mandls had the only petrol pump in the district. Herr Mandl was a friendly, rather stout man with red cheeks . . .

'Oh yes, so he did.'

. . . who always put a little extra on the scales after weighing things out. We passed the shop every Sunday after church, and he would give us a sweet each for the way home. It lasted exactly as long as it took us to reach our own front door.

'Yes, that's right,' said Agnes. 'Our shop was closed on Sundays, but he made an exception for the Count's family. My father did everything he could for them,' she said, looking at us and smiling radiantly. Wasn't what we were doing wrong? But I read on, about the train from Budapest, and how you saw it coming from far away because of its sooty smoke in the air, and about the cranes at the way into the village. I read the harmless passages, and skipped the rest.

19

What, I wondered on the way back to my hotel, past bakeries and dimly lit bars where men stood in front of fruit machines, ignoring the cigarette ash on their trousers, what distinguished my grandmother's parents from Aunt Margit? My great-grandparents watched as the Mandls were shot, and did all they could to hush up the crime, and in Rechnitz, just before the end of the war, Margit was dancing while 180 people fell into a grave that they had been forced to dig for themselves.

It was late afternoon, and it had indeed stopped raining; the asphalt was dry in many places. I had headphones on, and went past the hotel, going along the streets instead as if I were mowing a lawn, four blocks to the left, up another, then four blocks back. They were not bloodthirsty monsters. My relations had not tortured or shot anyone. They had simply watched and done nothing, they had stopped thinking, they had stopped existing as human beings although they knew what was going on. Is that, in Hannah Arendt's famous phrase, the banality of evil? I asked myself as I walked and walked, feeling that I never wanted to stop putting one foot in front of another. Everyone knew all about it, I murmured to myself. Passers by, looking at me, might have thought I was humming along to a song, but I was thinking of a passage in the book *Von den Flammen verzehrt* [Consumed by Flames], by the journalist Lilly Kertész, a Hungarian from the town of Eger, who had been deported to Auschwitz in 1944. She describes her neighbours looking down into the yard and watching as the Jews were taken away. 'You won't be coming back,' they shouted as music and laughter came from their apartments, and she was surprised. 'I knew the people who lived in that building. They had always seemed friendly to me.'

The far right Arrow Cross party could no longer keep up with the killing in the winter months of 1944. The trains were full, so they sent tens of thousands of Jews and Roma gypsies on death marches, driven by Hungarian gendarmes, who whipped them on for up to thirty kilometres a day; every fifth prisoner died. Everyone could see that from their windows too; they stood behind the lace curtains and watched the parade. What did they do then? Make soup, go to bed early?

And what about all the people who watched the Jews of Budapest – women, children, the old – chained together by handcuffs as they fell into the ice-cold Danube? Only the one at the end of the chain had to be shot, and then they would all be dragged into the river after that first one. Why didn't the passers by begin to scream? Why didn't the people in their fine apartments fling themselves down on their backs and kick furiously like babies? Why did they all take it so calmly? For the sake of law and order? For fear of losing their self-control?

20

I ought to have ordered a taxi, I thought as we drove past the last high-rise buildings in the city centre, but I had been too cowardly to refuse the offer when Marga and her husband said they would take me to the airport. All the time we had been in the car, Marga dwelt on the subject of her mother Agnes and our afternoon with her yesterday. 'She couldn't have coped with the truth,' she said, raising her voice so that it sounded like a question. Her husband put his hand on her knee. 'Let it rest, Marga. We've discussed it, after all.'

'And wasn't it lovely to see her like that?' she asked, turning to me. She did not hide the tears that were running down her face. What was I to reply? I was sitting on the back seat, and retreated into the corner. As if I were injured, that was how I sat there, as if I were in flight.

I was holding a slim volume that the two sisters had given me as a goodbye present. A few years ago, Agnes had met a historian in the Shoah Museum of Buenos Aires, and had asked him to help her write down her memories of the war years. I planned to read it on the flight.

'I think it was the right thing to do,' I heard myself saying to Marga, and I looked out of the window because I didn't want to see her tears.

The three of us stood in line for me to check in my case, talking about the cramped rows of seats in economy class, the bad films, the airline food. I felt like a child when he first time leaves his parents for a long time; I could have embraced them. I imagined what it would feel like to put my head on their bony shoulders, but that wouldn't do; we hardly knew each other. Later we drank coffee on the first floor of the departures hall. Marga was holding a handkerchief, asked me once again to send copies of the diary, and once again I said I would. And when I finally went through security, and turned for the last time, I waved like a good little boy. Why, I wondered, did I want them to remember me as someone showing humility?

Because they were victims?

What was I, then – one of the perpetrators?

*

Seven years had passed since I read that newspaper story about Rechnitz, saw the photo of Aunt Margit, and began investigating the history of my family. What was it all in aid of?

I imagined my father asking, 'Does it do any good?'

No, of course it doesn't, I felt like shouting back. By comparison with, say, the discovery of antibiotics it does no good at all.

So what, I asked myself, is going on? It was a question that I was always asking, usually when I was alone, in trains, in cafés, on entering a new hotel room when you push the curtain aside and look out of the window – what is going on? I sat by a window on the aircraft, drinking tomato juice, the reading light shone down from the ceiling on the folding table in front of me, with the diaries of Agnes and my grandmother lying on it. A lonely light above the black Atlantic, 10,000 metres above sea level, that was what it felt like. A Swiss couple were sitting beside me. They wore identical trousers, weatherproofed and supplied with all manner of zips, above, below, everywhere you could open, raise or adjust something, depending on whether the weather was wet or sunny. They've probably been climbing two or three glaciers in Tierra del Fuego, I thought, and then spent a few days in the desert, and finally a lazy week in the Mendoza vineyards. There was dried mud in the grooved soles of their hiking boots, and I couldn't take my eyes off them. Out of the corner of my eye, I looked at the small beard under the man's lower lip, a little patch of bristles trimmed precisely to the nearest milli-metre and looking just like the Velcro fastener on his jacket. Every time the couple said something to each other, they kissed, which made me want to tear their heads off. Why I don't know. Why did their harmony infuriate me? Why did I feel such contempt for those trousers, symbolizing their confidence that all the world's problems could be solved with the aid of zips and Velcro fasteners?

Why do I dislike this couple? I wrote in my notebook, not knowing what else to do. What have they ever done to me? I decided to look at that question with Strassberg.

Are you envious? I asked myself, writing it down. Envious of what?

I remembered going to Italy on holiday with friends, years ago. We had hardly any money, we slept out of doors, lit campfires and grilled meat over them, our car broke down, we went for a week without showering, and when it was time to go home, through the Gotthardt tunnel with the mountains behind us, past bottle-green lakes with white swans on them, past large farmhouses and cows bursting with good health, one of us said, 'Switzerland is the most beautiful country, after all.' I could have throttled him. Even then, I felt as much alone in my sorrow as I did now in the plane, beside the happy Swiss couple who couldn't wait to get home.

Was I envious of their feeling that they had a place where every-thing was all right, and you didn't need to have any doubts? Was that it?

Yes, maybe. And I watched them eating their sandwiches, crumbs getting caught in the little hairs of their fleece jackets, while they clicked through their holiday photographs. 'That's Tupungato,' I heard him saying. 'Are you sure?' she asked, kissing him again. 'Yes, of course – look at the striking flank of the mountain.' He kissed her back.

185

I put on my headphones and tuned into the classical music channel. Chopin, that would be fine, or at least it sounded fine. The light now falling on the two women's diaries from above was like a spotlight directed at a stage. I suddenly saw a room full of people from different periods before me, some wearing trainers and headphones, others in uniforms – the uniforms of the German Wehrmacht, the NKVD, the Hungarian police, they were all there. I saw my wife and my children, no escaping it now, I saw Linda the prostitute with her dog, Strassberg smoking his pipe with a gloomy expression, he didn't seem happy with all this. I saw Böhme and Simanovsky, sitting a row in front of Agnes and talking like the best of friends. Someone coughed, someone else cleared his throat. 'Come on, then,' said the writer Maxim Biller scornfully, 'what's that to do with you?'

What indeed.

It has something to do with a lack of honesty, that much is clear to me now. That is where it all connects up – in human failure.

I don't recognize myself in my Aunt Margit's hunger for power. Certainly not in her Nazi sympathies. I don't recognize myself in either my grandmother's mourning for feudal Hungary or her longing for home and good order. But I do recognize myself in her weaknesses.

Would I have acted differently from my grandmother on that afternoon long ago? Would I have opposed a father who didn't want to step in and do something? Would I have kept him from hushing up the murders? Have I ever really opposed anything? No, why would I? After all, everything in Switzerland is just fine, I hear myself replying.

Is it?

Of course I was against it when the Americans marched into Iraq. I was against conservative policies on immigration. Against the slaughter of dolphins in the Bay of Taiji. And when demonstrations began, not by chance, when I was fetching the children from kindergarten, I was often out on the streets myself, protesting. These days we spend hours on Facebook and Twitter, supporting or opposing this or that, sharing photos of bloodshed and clever analyses, linking to videos of shipwrecks with migrants drowning off Lampedusa, signing virtual petitions against female genital mutilation in South Sudan. But how would we act if these events moved from our computers to the street outside? If demands were made of us as human beings, not users of the media, if it were all physical instead of virtual? If it stank, hurt, was noisy, and we couldn't perceive the world through the restrained design of our Apple laptops. If there was war of the same kind as seventy years ago, wouldn't we all be fellow travellers?

Of course not, the young with their trainers and their jute bags would protest. We've all learnt from the past. That couldn't happen to us.

Couldn't it?

Aren't we suddenly obedient and aware of our duty when it comes to saving our own skins? Aren't we Simanovskys and Böhmes, don't we all have a little of Margit in us?

We are not prison warders, we don't carry out interrogations, we don't have people shot either, but how do we act in confrontations much less dangerous than wars? In the office, for example, when we want to show ourselves in a good light? Are we honest enough to speak the truth, even when the truth is uncomfortable? Have we protected people bullied by our bosses – or have we stood watching, like the passers by in Budapest when the Jews drowned in the Danube? Would we have stood up for them because they were suffering injustice, or would we have kept quiet, like my grandmother? Would we have taken a personal risk? Do we ever accept risks at all? Who will take a risk, and what for?

We sit on platforms, we write blogs, earn applause, shake hands, donate money, visit psychoanalysts, wax virtually indignant about the endangered mangrove swamps, the refusal to accept Nigerian refugees, thus pleasing maybe 107 readers and getting invited to join new networks – Xing, Pinterest, LinkedIn – where we come upon profiles of our friends and are surprised, damn it all, at what they're all reading and where they're all going: to Phnom Penh, Detroit, TED conferences, the Burning Man festival and the art fairs of Art Basel.

But has anyone ever tweeted about his weaknesses, shared fears, blogged about doubts, confessed that he isn't interested in the Muslim minority in Burma, said he doesn't want to know about the mangroves and he wasn't brave enough to tell his boss what he thought?

Are we really as squeaky-clean as we present ourselves virtually? How steadfast are we? How steadfast am I?

I opened my notebook, read the date that I had entered in the departures hall of the airport before takeoff, top left on a new page, and wrote: 'Could you have done it – could you have hidden Jews?' And under it the answer. 'No.'

21

Aweek later I was lying on Strassberg's couch again. I had been looking forward to our first session after my journey to Argentina. I would really have liked him to go to Buenos Aires with me, and then we could have met every evening in one of those grill restaurants, to drink the heavy Malbec wine that leaves blood-red marks at the corners of your mouth. Then we could have talked about everything. Now I didn't know where to begin.

'Well,' I said after a while, 'it was curiously harmonious.'

'It was?'

'Even before we met it was like that. On the phone and in our emails, we felt that familiarity. And when I saw Agnes's two daughters in the restaurant for the first time, they said how good it was that we were meeting in person, and how close they felt to me, as if we'd known each other for ages – and I felt so too. But all the same . . .'

'Yes?'

'Hard to say.'

Strassberg said nothing.

'When they asked me if I could copy those pages of the diary for them, I hesitated. I didn't want to. Not yet, I haven't reached that point. It's all still too raw and unfinished in my mind. I mean, it's my story too. I've no idea what they'd make of it.'

'That's the point.'

'What point?'

'Power over the story. It was already about that for your

grandmother, and for her father when he hushed up the murder. And it's the same now for you and Agnes's daughters: who's going to decide what the end of the story is?'

'Hmm,' I said.

'I deliberately didn't say that before you flew to Argentina because I didn't want to influence you,' he went on. 'But where your relationship to Agnes's daughters is concerned, you're in a difficult position: you can only lose. If you don't do exactly what they ask, you'll soon find yourself on the side of the villains. It wouldn't surprise me if the harmony you mentioned comes to a rapid end.'

*

In April, I came across Linda again, the tart I had met in the train with her dog. I saw her by chance in a side street near the railway station. I wasn't sure at first, and followed her for a few metres. She was with another woman, their shoulders touching, and they wore long, black quilted jackets that went down to their knees, although it was a pleasantly warm day. I was right behind them now, and heard their Hungarian, which sounded so different from the language as my father spoke it, darker, rougher. I hesitated to speak to her, because what did I want from her? However, in the end I did call out, 'Linda,' whereupon she turned and looked at me in surprise. She was wearing hardly any make-up and looked smaller than I remembered her; I saw a cold sore on her lower lip. 'Do you remember me?' I asked, but she shook her head. 'We met on the train to Budapest late last year,' I said. 'We were sitting next to each other, and you had a dog with you.' Now she nodded, and her friend cast her an inquiring glance. They were both smoking those long, thin cigarettes with white filters that look from a distance like drinking straw. I've seen them smoked only by women from the East.

'What luck,' I said, because I couldn't think of the Hungarian for 'what a coincidence'. Wasn't that too pushy, I wondered? 'Do you have time for a coffee?' I asked her and her friend. I couldn't think of anything better.

They shook their heads. 'Why?' they said.

'Just asking,' I replied. As in the night train to Budapest, Linda was not unfriendly, only cautious.

'I'd like to talk to you both.'

'What about?'

'About your lives, and about Hungary.'

They looked at each other, laughed, and both threw their cigarettes away at the same time, to roll under a car. Their lives were boring, and Hungary was a shitty country, said Linda. They looked at one another again. 'We could have a bite to eat too,' I suggested. 'Sounds okay to me,' said Linda, without looking me in the face. We crossed the street and went into a Turkish snack bar that smelled of onions and soap, and sat in the corner in front of mirror walls. Both women kept looking in the mirrors as they smoothed down their hair. They placed their phones on the table beside them as if they were pistols.

'Why is Hungary a shitty country?' I asked after a while. Linda's friend Marika didn't talk much. She was younger, hardly twenty, had black, almost shoulder-length hair falling over a birthmark on her throat. She laughed when Linda laughed, and often answered at the same time.

'Because there's no work in Hungary. Because life there is no good,' said Linda.

'I understand.'

'You understand what?'

We fell silent.

'What sort of work do you do?' they asked.

'I'm a journalist. I write.'

'What were you doing in Hungary?'

'Visiting my father. And I went to a little village called Sárosd, do you know it?' Then I began telling them about it. About my journey, and my grandmother's diary. The waiter brought our food. I mentioned the crime that had been committed in the castle courtyard. 'A Jewish married couple were shot there a year before the end of the Second World War,' I said, watching Linda and Marika eating their kebabs, which were dripping with yoghurt sauce. I must have sounded like a confused old man; I saw nothing but surprise in their faces.

'Second World War?' repeated Marika solemnly, as if it were something from classical antiquity that had to be wrapped in silk to protect it from direct sunlight.

'Yes,' I said. They picked up the onions that fell from the flatbreads to their plates in their long fingernails, which they used like chopsticks.

'But that's a hundred years ago.'

'Seventy,' I corrected her, like a teacher, but what difference did it make? We went on eating without saying much, and I felt ridiculous, because in a few hours' time they would be standing outside those compartments in the old garages waiting for customers, and here was I telling them a story that had happened decades ago in my grandmother's family's courtyard, back in a world that was dead and gone now. I helped them to tear open the little white bags with freshen-up tissues that the waiter brought us, whereupon the whole place smelled of lemon, and then we stood up and went outside. They wanted a cigarette rather than coffee, stood in front of the yellow wall by the entrance, and looked for lighters in their jackets.

'Do your parents know what you girls are doing in Zürich?' I asked.

Marika shook her head.

'Do you work in those compartments?'

'Are you going to write about us?' asked Linda.

'May I?'

Linda said, 'My father left. My mother is at home with my daughter. Will that do?' She blew the first smoke from her cigarette out through her nose. 'A photo would be good,' I said, reaching into my pocket. 'I'll murder you if you do that,' said Linda, avoiding my eyes. 'I haven't done my face, so I look like a pancake.' I wanted to say something nice in reply, but couldn't think of anything in Hungarian.

'Some women tell their daughters about it,' she said.

'You don't?'

'No.'

'You could warn her.'

'We all have to look out for ourselves.'

'As a child, I'd want to know what my mother did.'

'What are you talking about?' She smoked, looked at the ground, and began telling me about her village, and the other gypsy girls who tie plastic bottles or bits of silver foil to the branches of trees beside the highways, so that they will shine in the sunlight and the truck drivers will see them far off. In summer the girls wait in the bushes beside the road, until one of them brakes and gets out, groans as he comes, pays, and drives off again. Some took the girls a few kilometres on, telling their colleagues by radio that they had a girl with them, slender or plump, brunette or blonde, and so they were passed on from driver to driver, like the baton in a relay race, going westwards with one driver and southwards with another, all across the country; sometimes they were dumped at a service station like a dog who has turned out to be a nuisance, and if they got pregnant that was too bad. 'That's how it starts,' said Linda, objectively, and she signed to Marika that it was time for them to go. We said goodbye, I wrote my number on two scraps of paper – 'Call if you need anything,' I said, but I knew that they wouldn't. Then we shook hands.

'What happened to your dog?' I called after her. Linda shook her head.

*

'I didn't tell you that on my journey to Hungary last autumn I met a prostitute,' I told Daniel Strassberg a week later, when I was on his couch.

193

'No,' he said.

'I got talking to her in the train, and then by chance I saw her again a few days ago. We went and had something to eat. She and a girlfriend of hers, they're both from Hungary, from a small village. Now they stand in front of the compartments where the tarts do business, waiting for customers. I told them about the diary, about the Mandls, and how I went to see the castle.'

'Why?'

'I don't know. I wanted to tell them something about me. Maybe I also wanted to see how they'd react. The double lives of people like Linda have always fascinated me: what do they tell their mothers at home? What do they do when their daughters ask questions? How often do they think about what's really going on?'

'What do the double lives of those prostitutes have to do with you?'

'Nothing, really,' I replied, looking past Leibniz and Lacan, and up to the wooden figure on the shelf. Someone had turned her round, so that I saw her back view, her large, wide hips. 'Or rather, yes, it does have something to do with me. it's about the question of how much of ourselves we disclose. What stories do we admit to? What kind of truth about ourselves do we construct? What do we pass on and what would we rather keep quiet? It was only at the end of her life that my grandmother decided to open up, and Agnes's daughters are going to keep the true version of their grandparents' death to themselves, just as Linda won't be telling her family about soliciting customers from those compartments, and what it feels like to go back and stand in line after getting out of the last customer's car, with some of his sperm left in her mouth.'

Strassberg did not reply to that.

'There's still the question . . .'

'Yes?'

'What about me?'

'What do you mean?'

'How does my own story run? What am I going to pass on, and what will I keep to myself?'

'You decided on psychoanalysis, so it looks as if you're confronting your weaknesses.'

'Casting light on the dark places? But is that really what I'm doing?'

'How did those two women react to what you said about your grandmother's diary?'

'They thought I was crazy. We went to eat kebabs, and I talked to them about the Second World War, which was absurd. I seemed to myself incredibly old, because it's all so long ago, and at the same time incredibly young and naïve and spoilt, like one of those pale students at a top English university who know life only from books. I've been lying on your couch for years, racking my brains over the past, while Linda and Marika are fighting for their present every day.' I stopped, because I didn't know how to go on, and lay there for some minutes without saying a word. 'Don't you think I ought simply to throw my earlier life overboard like ballast, the way balloonists do?' I asked.

He did not reply and once again I had the feeling that I was just talking nonsense.

'Then I'd be setting my own course,' I went on, all the same. 'I'd be carrying less weight, I'd gain height. Do you remember the bond my grandmother talked about, the bond between her and us, grandparents and grandchildren?'

'Yes.'

'I'm not sure whether it shouldn't be cut. Then one could begin again, and not be weighed down by the burden of the past. Although what's the point? We can't deny our own roots and throw our past out with the garbage, or can we? I suppose we have to start by understanding where we come from and who we are before we can start again, do you think that's it? And only someone who sees that bond ahead of him first, shining like the lights that mark out the landing strips of airports at night, can then cut it. Oh, let's drop the subject for today. It's not so important.'

'There you go saying that again.'

'Saying what again?'

'I think it's all important, or you wouldn't be here. Maybe you should stop dismissing everything to do with yourself as unimportant. You're not doing anyone down if you stand up for your own concerns.'

'I don't understand.'

'Nor do I, entirely. But we have time.'

*

In September, I finally sat down at my desk and drew the curtains over the window. I had designed a diagram to give me a survey of the whole story; I had tried to sum up all my travels and researches in it, with arrows and lines and symbols for the various characters: my father the moon, my grandmother a circle, Agnes a bird – and Margit's symbol was the swastika. I cut out the diagram and pinned it up on the wall in front of me, adjusted my chair, and began writing. I went on and on every day without stopping. The first month went all right; I typed without noticing that the days were getting shorter and shorter. The first leaves fell off the trees, my children needed new gumboots. In the second month I was cursing muself; in the third month I realized that you can't write about your own psychoanalysis while it's still going on, because you'd have to keep going back to the subject of earlier sessions, whereupon everything would change. You can't put what goes on in those sessions into words, and if you do the whole thing falls apart in front of your eyes. In the fourth month snow fell for days on end, boots with warm linings took over from the gumboots, and I came to the conclusion that I had to go on one last journey.

22

There was one passage in my grandmother's diary where I had doubted the veracity of what she said. Soon after the shooting of the Mandls, she wrote that she had set off for the camp where Agnes and Sándor were being held. She told her parents that she was going to Budapest to run a few errands there, but she did not mention the real reason for her journey.

German troops had occupied Hungary a few months earlier, Wehrmacht trucks were driving all over the country, the Arrow Cross right-wing party was on patrol, the Hungarian government under Döme Sztójay, the new prime minister and a Nazi sympathizer, had announced the founding of ghettoes, and Jews were obliged to wear the yellow star. Eichmann was stationed in Budapest, and had brought his entire staff. His Special Operation commando consisted of experienced men like Franz Novak and Dieter Wisliceny; Hitler had helped to pick them. Eichmann moved into a suite in the Hotel Astoria, where he met the Jewish Council of Budapest for the first time on 31 March. 'Do you know what I am?' he is said to have asked the assembled company, which included the president of the council Samuel Stern, and he will have waited for Stern to shake his head before replying, 'A bloodhound.' Over the next two months he sent 437,402 Jewish men and women, children and old people to Auschwitz. Most of them went straight from the ramp to the gas chambers.

It was at this time, then, that my grandmother went by train from her little village to Budapest, and on from there to Kistarcsa, where the camp was. She was 22 years old and pregnant with her second son, who was not to survive the following spring. She left her first child, my father, behind with her parents. She had to change trains in Budapest, passing the soldiers and wounded men on the East Station, in air full of soot and steam from the locomotives. Arriving on the platform, she sat down on a bench to wait, a young woman of good family from the country. I wonder how she was dressed? Not too elegantly, I am sure; she was on her way to a prison, and she never thought much about her clothes. Perhaps she wore a hat? Perhaps she had a little bag, and in the bag there was a notebook in which she was writing down, with the stump of a pencil, what she would say to Agnes, when a voice from the loudspeaker in the background announced that her train was coming in.

But now Agnes's daughters had told me that it really did happen like that. That my grandmother did indeed go to Kistarcsa, to see Agnes and Sándor. Why had it been so hard for me to believe her?

Because I didn't think her capable of it, that was why. It wasn't her courage that surprised me but her determination, her strength and her self-confidence. After all, this was the woman who had described herself more than once in her diary as a mole, *head down underground, always ducking out of sight.*

Years ago, my father had told me that every two weeks a stranger with a case on wheels rang my grandmother's doorbell and pressed her to buy a new fire extinguisher. Stacks of them soon accumulated in the cellar. She wasn't senile, she knew it was a confidence trick, but she didn't send him away because she didn't have the nerve to snub him. She would rather not claim her human rights than defend herself, she would rather listen to his lecture on the advantages of the new kind of extinguishing foam than slam the door in the face of this stranger in his ill-fitting suit. The salesman obviously sensed that, and was exploiting it. That was how she had been brought up; she always put herself and her own needs last, she would finish up stale bread rather than buy fresh, and when it came to making space for herself, maybe using her elbows in the super-market, she crept away. Restraint was her idea of good behaviour.

I found it all the more remarkable, then, that she went to that camp in secret seventy years ago. It was the only time in her life, so far as I knew, that she did not go along with other people. On that day she threw off everything that was part of her character, all the baggage she brought with her, her shame, the pain of the era then ending, the laissez-faire attitude of her social class. She overcame the weariness that affected all of Hungary at the time, the resigna-tion that had afflicted the country since the end of the monarchy and plunged the people into bloodshed. With her journey to the camp, she was also opposing her father and the village priest, both of whom had hushed up the crime against the Mandls. She shed her second skin, the skin of the mole, sat naked in that train and looked out of the window, driven on by the will to do something at last.

That was why I, too, was going to the town where the camp stood to pay her tribute, to be close to her at that moment of her life. And yes, perhaps I also wanted some of the strength that had sur-rounded her at the time for myself.

A half-litre beer can rolled on the floor at my feet as the train began moving away from Budapest, past Ikea and McDonald's, past the hoardings with advertisements and the prefabricated buildings on the outskirts of the city. What would she have seen at the time? Fields with some snow still lying on them, a horse-drawn plough, a single poppy beside a road, a tank at a crossing and soldiers, soldiers everywhere. The beer can rolled back again, and past me once more when the train next stopped. It was a chilly Saturday morning in December, all you saw of the sun was a bright ring, the rest of it was hidden behind thick clouds. The heating under my seat hummed. Two elderly women sat opposite me, complaining about their pension contributions; I looked past them at the turquoise upholstery of the seats with its strange pattern, a jagged bundle of assorted colours, lightning flashes pointing in all directions. Who, I wondered as the women went on to discuss the price of gas in the last year, would come up with an idea like that? Someone must have designed that pattern, the way the lines went, someone had sat at a computer for nights on end over it. There must have been discussions, presentations, and at a certain point that person had been given the go-ahead and was delighted. There are human beings behind all decisions, whether they concern the upholstery of train seats or compartments where prostitutes deal with their customers; there was always someone who said, 'This is how we'll do it.' I always found that a fascinating idea.

We passed the little Mátyásföld airfield. Had there been planes with swastikas on their sides standing on the runway then? Did she imagine what it would be like when she stood at the camp gate? Had she prepared something to say? Did she have money to bribe the soldiers with her? Did she hope to buy freedom for Agnes – or to atone for her own guilt?

*

The Kistarcsa camp has existed since the 1920s. Originally it was a textiles factory with over a thousand workers, for whom dormitories had been built on the other side of the tracks. But the factory suffered severely in the international economic crisis of 1929, and the Interior Ministry took it over and converted it into a prison. At the time, the idea of a healthy body politic that must be guarded from harmful influences reigned in Hungary, and it meant living in zones: the good people in one place while the bad belonged behind bars. Up to the Second World War, the buildings were used to hold communists, criminals, homosexuals, the mentally sick, people who were a nuisance and did not fit into the picture. The place was already being compared with Auschwitz, both of them former factories outside large cities and connected to a railway network, which was practical. There were no locals apart from a few farmers, who acted as if they didn't notice what was going on, there were few witnesses, and hardly any danger of inmates escaping. Today it would be called a 'black site'. Kistarcsa was a place that no one knew.

When the Germans marched into Hungary on 19 March 1944, the camp fell into the hands of the SS, who filled it with Jews to be deported to Auschwitz. And when the communists came to power in 1948, and Mátyás Rákosi carried out the orders issued by Stalin in Moscow, it was the political opponents of the regime – a few aristocrats, many churchmen – who were held in the same cells as Agnes and her brother Sándor before them. Guards and inmates came and went; Kistarcsa stayed put. By the time of the uprising against Russian rule in 1956, thousands of people had been imprisoned there. There were no beds, hardly any blankets, no hope of a fair trial. Among the inmates was Cardinal Mindszenty, head of the Hungarian Catholic Church, who had the courage to criticize the regime of the Arrow Cross party from his pulpit, and later also denounced the equally inhumane communist system. But unlike Mindszenty himself, Kistarcsa survived even that.

In the early eighties a few of the rooms there were used for police training, others stood empty. These were perhaps the most peaceful years that the place saw, in a frozen time behind the Iron Curtain, until the fall of the Berlin Wall turned everything upside down once more, and the real purpose of Kistarcsa was remembered. Soon the cells were full again, the guards had bunches of keys at their belts and cudgels in their hands, mashed potato was slapped down on plates in the canteen as before. Kistarcsa was back in business, now as one of the largest transit camps in Europe. After the Jews, after the opponents of communism, it was now the turn of black people, the destitute and starving to be held here – pests who must be kept at bay. Before being deported, around 20,000 people, mainly from Africa, spent a few months in these cells, where the entire history of European brutality in the last century was reflected.

*

The very last inmates of the camp were eighteen migrants from Rwanda. They had fled over the mountains of former Yugoslavia, where they almost froze to death, after losing their friends and families while crossing the Mediterranean, and of course they had no idea where they had ended up. The dormitories and dining rooms were empty, there was no one else around apart from a few guards waiting out their time here, and members of a refugee organization who brought in fruit and told the puzzled cook not to put pork in his watery goulash. Plaster had been flaking off the walls for ages, the toilets didn't work, roots of trees pushed up through the tarmac of the paths between the buildings. The Rwandans did what all the inmates before them had done: they waited, they smoked, they slept poorly. They were the final remnants, the last in a long line of people who had been locked up here until, one day, they were expelled over the border to Serbia, the same way as they had come. Or perhaps they were flown back to Kigali in handcuffs, who knows?

The buildings had been standing empty for ten years. Some had been torn down, others rebuilt, a kindergarten moved in. Where people had once been imprisoned before being taken to Auschwitz, there was now a school financed by the European Union. *Magyarország megújul*, 'Hungary Renewed', said a panel in front of the entrance, the place was gleaming with varnish, the windows were double-glazed, looking through them, you could see children sitting at low tables.

I walked along the streets of this small town, maybe much as my grandmother had done years ago, looking for a gate, an entrance. I noticed the memorials scattered around the town, six or seven of them: a marble slab erected to the victims of the Second World War, a wooden memorial for the victims of Communism, a white stone commemorating the Trianon peace treaty of 1920. In Hungary, evil always comes from outside, whether by way of the Germans, the Russians, the Allies – that was the message conveyed to every visitor to the Budapest museums. Hungary was always the victim, Hungary was always innocent. But wasn't that camp the real monument to the area? Shouldn't at least a couple of its walls have been retained, so that no one would forget what cruel things Hungarian prison guards did over a century? The country might have renewed itself, as the panel outside the kindergarten claimed, but what was left of the past, what story was told here?

At a crossroads, I fell into conversation with an old woman who told me what it had looked like here sixty years ago. She pointed her stick at various buildings. 'That one, that one and that one weren't here yet,' she said. 'Or that, or that.'

'But the camp was here instead,' I interrupted her.

'Oh yes, the camp.' She looked down at the ground.

I helped her with her shopping bags – one of them had leeks sticking out of it – and we walked to her home. 'I know someone who was in the camp,' I said awkwardly, to which she nodded, but she said no more about it, and asked no questions. 'There must have been a gate to it somewhere?' I asked.

'It's a long way off.' Beyond the station, she said, she was sure I'd have to walk for half an hour to get there. I left the shopping bags outside her front door, pulled my cap down over my ears, and set off. Five minutes later I had reached the camp gate. How could the old woman have been so wrong? Because all anyone could do was push the camp away from them, was that it? Pushing it a little farther away every year, until in the end it disappeared entirely. Just as there are said to be people in Germany who live near former concentration camps and grow geraniums in their window boxes, and if you ask them whether it doesn't bother them, living here, they ask why it would.

I held on to the green railings surrounding the buildings. Had my grandmother stood here as well? She doesn't say much about it in her diary; she will have been nervous, scared, and she will have felt frozen because even in summer she felt cold in the shade of large trees, but there was no stopping her. It was as if everything depended on that meeting. *I must talk to Agi*, she wrote, and how I wished I could see her face at that time, her eyes, her mouth. Was she smoking? Hastily inhaling the smoke before she approached the soldier at the gate? No, that can't be right; she was pregnant, and also it wasn't proper for young ladies to smoke in the street – but so what? Hadn't she rejected such ideas by coming here? She was no longer a lady that day, that was it, at last she was a human being.

The camp was near the railway racks. I can remember meadows round it, and a gate guarded by a soldier in uniform, I don't know what his rank was. I didn't have any practice in deciphering military badges. I asked him whether Agnes and Sándor Mandl, a sister and brother, were in the prison, and if I could speak to them – it was important. He made a note of my request. He wasn't uncivil, in fact he was very nice.

From where I was standing by the railings, I could see into some of the rooms through the broken windows; there was scribbles on the walls, and graffiti on the outer walls of the building, and I was reminded of Simon and his friends, about whom I had written a column years ago. They were a group of British young people who spent their weekends exploring factories that had been shut down, abandoned sanatoriums for the mentally sick, uninhabited castles quietly mouldering away. They didn't break in like burglars, they were well prepared and did not vandalize these places, they had got hold of plans from the land registry office, and knew the shafts of the sewage system through which we spent a whole morning crawling, seeing dead rats in the light from our headlamps, and finally coming up through the heating shaft in the laundry of a sanatorium. Once there, they looked through old files, lay on mildewed mattresses, and took photos of the padded cells. They talked all day about what it must have felt like back when depressives and schizophrenics were treated by electric shock therapy. I felt at ease with Simon and his friends. I understood their liking for what has been forgotten, I shared their sense of the aesthetics of decay, and all of that now came back to my mind as I stood outside the nicotine-yellow walls of the camp.

Diaries VI

Maritta

I must have waited for two hours outside the camp gate. I walked a few steps up and down, wondering what I was going to say to Agi and Sándor when I saw them.

Agnes

One day a police officer came and said someone wanted to speak to me.

But I didn't trust him, and I was frightened to go with him. 'I tell you, there's someone for you,' he claimed. I shook my head, and he left the room.

Maritta

I thought they would be surprised to see me.

Agnes

Was there really someone looking for me? Who could it have been?

Maritta

When the soldier came back, he said there was no one of that name in the camp, so I went home. I had to change trains in Budapest, where the concourse in front of the station was teeming with soldiers and dogs and ambulances. The rooftops of the city centre shone in the light of the setting sun, and pollen was dancing in the air. I suddenly saw a woman who seemed very familiar to me, but I recognized her only when we were almost level with one another. She was the owner of the best perfumery in Budapest, an elderly lady whom I had seen only in her white coat at her place behind the counter. Now she had a Star of David on her dark jacket. But when I was about to go up to her, she passed me with her face averted. At that I ran to the nearest flower stall – I had to do something, I was so upset – and bought a yellow daffodil to put in my buttonhole. A German was coming towards me. I gave him as fierce a look as I could manage, but the German, clearly a high-ranking officer, said, 'Fabulous' – and bowed, with a smile. What a ridiculous demonstrator I made. A yellow daffodil instead of a Star of David. Was that the best I could do? Yes, it evidently was.

23

If my grandmother could have talked to Agi, how would she have begun the conversation, what would she have told her? I had already discussed that in Buenos Aires, with Agnes's daughters.

Would she have apologized? 'I'm sorry I stood by and did nothing while they shot your mother and father in the back.'

Would she have explained? 'We were too cowardly, I, my father, the family, the whole bloody aristocracy, we'd grown too self-satisfied and indifferent, if you see what I mean. We couldn't do it, couldn't act like human beings and hide Jews, we didn't take the risk. We are not a family of heroes, we're more like moles.'

And how would Agnes have reacted to the news? She was younger than my grandmother, and had no idea what was coming her way. She was alone, she had been separated from her brother, she had a photograph of her family with her, and the last thing her father had said to her was still ringing in her ears. 'What will become of you two?'

So what would she have done when my grandmother had confessed to the crime? It would probably have been the death of her; the will to live that Agnes still feels today – her daughters, too, kept telling me about it – would have been broken. She could hardly have survived Auschwitz without the hope of seeing her parents again. Unlike most of the women inmates, Agnes wrote, she had kept her strength for a long time, and as if miraculously was spared illnesses. It was only because the Germans considered her capable of working that she managed to survive. Suppose my grandmother's confession had taken that strength away from her? Did she think of that when she went to the camp? *I had to talk to Agnes,* she wrote, but what did she mean? Who was she thinking of most, Agnes or herself?

No doubt my grandmother would have felt better after confessing her guilt; wasn't that why people went to confession? Was it absolution that she wanted Agnes to give her? After that, she could have told her father that she was no longer going to cover up for his deception, and then she might have gone through life feeling more honest – two or three degrees more honest, no more. But that would have been enough for her to begin writing earlier, because it was what she always wanted to do, as she says in her diary: *writing is my only passion in life.* Only by writing, as she knew, could she fight back against her own extinction. Kistarcsa could have been a turning point in her life; she could have passed on to my father a few sparks of the new fire she felt, taught him to stand up to more physically, to have more confidence. And then he could have passed it on to me. Because that was why I had been lying on Strassberg's couch and talking all these years, so that I would finally exist, would finally leave footprints in the snow behind me. Did that afternoon in Kistarcsa perhaps affect me, too?

My grandmother's confession, while it might have revived our family, would have annihilated the Mandls; one could be had only at the cost of the other. So it was as well that the soldier had claimed neither Agnes nor Sándor was in that camp.

My grandmother must have stood on the station platform with her head bowed, waiting for the train, because she had not succeeded in speaking to Agnes, and her wish to confess had been thwarted. Now there was nothing she could do but go back to her father in the castle, back to the moles' burrow, and stay underground. So she let the following years pass over her – and it was Agnes who survived.

*

I went once around the buildings, keeping close to the railings, past young trees and bushes, heard the rustle of frozen leaves under my feet. I hoped to find a place where I could easily climb over to the other side. Then I would explore the dormitories, as I had in England with Simon and his friends in that sanatorium, I would see the toilets and touch the walls. Was the mortal fear of hundreds of thousands of people still perceptible if you walked through those empty rooms? I imagined what it would be like if the sounds inside the camp had been continuously recorded – what would we hear now, a hundred years of screaming? Or had they all been silenced by fear? Then I stopped and held my breath, as if a deer were staring at me and might leap away at the slightest movement. Didn't I fly to Argentina for the same reason as my grandmother had gone to Kistarcsa seventy years ago? We both wanted to tell Agnes the truth about the death of her parents. It was a new idea to me that we both had the same thing in mind, and we had both failed. She did not get into the camp, I did not get past the daughters who thought it would only hurt Agnes, just as it would have hurt her back then.

'Why did you come to Buenos Aires?' Mirta had asked me on the first evening, directly after I had read aloud to them from the diary. I had thought it was a case of embarrassment, and had been surprised. Our feelings were all so churned up, I thought, that she only wanted to bridge the silence, but now I realized there was more behind it – although why, in fact? I was a messenger, I had replied then, I wanted to bring them the story, but was I really doing it for Agnes and her family? Wasn't I, instead, doing it for myself?

I hadn't brought them anything, it now occurred to me, still frozen rigid. I hadn't given them anything; no, the fact was that I had taken something for myself. A scrap of existence. That is our secret pact in the later generations, whether we are descended from the victims or descended from the perpetrators. We all get something for ourselves, we dig for it as if it were a rare mineral, and we make it our own. At that point the deer ran away.

*

I walked around for a little longer, past a swimming pool, a Chinese restaurant; it was raining hard now, and I thought what it would have been like if my children had come on this expedition with me. My elder daughter had not even been one year old when I first went to Rechnitz; she was four when I visited Agnes in Buenos Aires, and soon she would be six.

'Papa, we're cold,' I could imagine them saying.

'But we have to see all the memorials,' I told them.

'Why bother?' they cried. 'We don't want to see any more.' And I nodded; yes, why bother? To get to the station I had to pass the camp again, following the railway tracks. It all lay open before me, all of the last hundred years; something that has always fascinated me about Hungary is that the history of the country can be seen on its roads, you could make your own picture of it, you could touch them, walk along them, you didn't need to go to a museum where they were kept to be shown in glass cases, where there were little lights and a chair for you to rest on in a corner. 'Do you understand that?' I asked my children in my thoughts, but they shook their heads. I saw my grandmother before me as I waited for the train on the platform, and looked round – somewhere nearby, Agnes must have been put on the train for Auschwitz.

My tears came without warning, they simply began to fall and merged with the raindrops on my face. I turned away so that no one else would see me weeping, turned up the collar of my coat and pulled my cap further down. It went on for minutes on end, and I did nothing to stop the tears until finally I was only retching, as if about to vomit, and that felt good. Then the train arrived.

I sat on the same upholstery, the brightly coloured lightning flashes on the turquoise background. I felt happy, I couldn't say why, and I suddenly felt sure that I ought to destroy my grandmother's diary as she had asked my father to do when she was dying. The book had fulfilled its purpose, I thought. I would take my children and my wife with me – I suddenly saw us all standing in a field under a grey sky, with a few ravens flying overhead, and we would take the pages closely written in my grandmother's handwriting, the pages that I had spent weeks deciphering, and throw them to the wind as if we were flying kites. Some sheets of paper would lie on the ground, others would get caught in the branches of trees, we would watch them fly away and laugh until the folder was empty. When the train began to move, the heating under my seat came on, and warm air crept into my wet coat.

ACKNOWLEDGEMENTS

I thank the UBS Culture Foundation, the Goethe Institute of Zürich and the Literature Foundation of Zürich for their generous support of my work on this book.

My thanks also go to my editor Martin Breitfeld, who urged me on and received a few grey hairs in return; to Silke Pfeiffer for her tireless work on the text, to Dieter Bacher for his help with Russian documents, and to Ritva Hämäläinen for translating them. Thanks to Paul Gulda for his early research tips, to Daniel Strassberg for so much, to the Kupferminc family for their warmth, to Bruno Augsburger for the nicest flat in the world, and to Finn Canonica of the *Tages-Anzeiger*, where reporting about my great-aunt Margit first appeared, for the leave he granted me. I am grateful to Christoph Zürcher from the NZZ *am Sonntag* for his valuable tips on storytelling and Miklós Gimes for his views on the true drama of life. To my parents I am thankful for everything – too much to put into words – and I am also grateful to my parents-in-law for their valuable help in the last few not entirely stress-free years. Lastly I am thankful to my two brothers for always being there for me and for allowing me to write down this story: for it is also their story.

My greatest thanks and my limitless love however goes to Suleika, who kept me going on days when I could barely speak more than five words, and without whom this book would not exist.